We Mark Your Memory

Writings from the Descendants of Indenture

COLONIAL EMIGRATION FORM No. 44.

MAN'S
EMIGRATION PASS.

HEALTH CLASS.

Depôt No. *1259*

For Ship *"Hereford"* .... PROCEEDING TO FIJI.

No. *443*

Fiji Government Emigration Agency,
12, Garden Reach, Kiddespore,

CALCUTTA, the *24/3* 189 *4*.

Particu-Lars of Regis-tration. { Place,	*Allahabad*
Date,	*6/3/94*
No. in Register	*269*
Name,	*Jaman Khan*
Father's Name,	*Din Mohamed*
Age,	*20*
Caste,	*Pathan*
Name of next-of-kin,	*Jhabbe, aunt*
If married, name of wife,	—
District,	*Cawnpur*
Thana,	*Rely Godam*
Village or Town & Mahalla,	*Siki Mohal*
Bodily Marks,	*Scar on right side of back,*
Height,	*5* Feet *4* Inches.

CERTIFIED that we have examined and passed the above named Man as fit
to emigrate ; that he is free from all bodily and mental disease ; and that he has
been vaccinated since engaging to emigrate.

DATED

The

_____
Surgeon Superintendent.

Depôt Surgeon.

CERTIFIED that the Man above described has appeared before me and has
been engaged by me on behalf of the Government of FIJI as willing to
proceed to that country to work for hire ; and that I have explained to him all
matters concerning his engagement and duties. This has also been done at the
time of registration by the registering officer appointed by the Indian Government.

DATED

The *12/3/94*

_____
Government Emigration Agent for FIJI.

PERMITTED to proceed as in a fit state of health to undertake the voyage to
FIJI.

DATED

The *27/11/94*

_____
Protector of Emigrants.

P. S. D'Rosario & Co., Printers, Calcutta,—1,000—12.93.

*The indenture certificate of the maternal great-grandfather of contributor Akhtar Mohammed
(Brotherhood of the Boat, p. 79).*

We Mark Your Memory

Writings from the Descendants of Indenture

edited by David Dabydeen, Maria del Pilar Kaladeen
and Tina K. Ramnarine

2018

School of Advanced Study
University of London

Commonwealth Writers

Published in Great Britain in 2018 by School of Advanced Study, University of London, in association with Commonwealth Writers

ISBN 978-1-912250-07-3

Cover image: Aquagraph image of Indians in Trinidad c.1915. One of a series of postcards by Raphael Tuck and Sons. For more information, please see https://tuckdb.org/about.

School of Advanced Study
University of London
Senate House
Malet Street
London WC1E 7HU
sas.publications@sas.ac.uk
www.sas.ac.uk/publications/

Contents

Introduction ix
*David Dabydeen, Maria del Pilar Kaladeen
and Tina K. Ramnarine*

Biographies xv

The Rebel 1
Kevin Jared Hosein

Mother Wounds 8
Gitan Djeli

Mama Liberia 25
Angelica A. Oluoch

My Father the Teacher 26
Prithiraj R. Dullay

Gandhi and the Girmitya 34
Satendra Nandan

Pepsi, Pie and Swimming Pools in-the-Sky 38
Cynthia Kistasamy

Escape from El Dorado: a bittersweet journey
through my Guyanese history 43
Anita Sethi

Talanoa with my Grandmother 50
Noelle Nive Moa

Passage from India 53
Anirood Singh

india has left us 69
Eddie Bruce-Jones

Chutney Love 71
Gabrielle Jamela Hosein

Brotherhood of the Boat: Fijians and Football in
North America 74
Akhtar Mohammed

The Heist 80
Deirdre Jonklaas Cadiramen

Buckets   87
Stella Chong Sing

The Tamarind Tree   90
Brij V. Lal

'I go sen' for you'   107
Fawzia Muradali Kane

Paradise Island   109
Priya N. Hein

Building Walls   114
Kama La Mackerel

The Legend of Nagakanna   120
Aneeta Sundararaj

Great-grandmother, Ma   127
Jennifer Rahim

Homecoming   130
Suzanne Bhagan

Erased   140
Athol Williams

Famished Eels   141
Mary Rokonadravu

Rights of Passage   149
Patti-Anne Ali

The Protest March that Ended Indian
Indentureship in St Vincent   153
Arnold N. Thomas

Sita and Jatayu   160
Lelawattee Manoo-Rahming

Tales of the Sea   162
Gaiutra Bahadur

Pot-bellied Sardar   175
David Dabydeen

Commonwealth Writers

Commonwealth Writers is the cultural initiative of the Commonwealth Foundation. It inspires and connects writers and storytellers across the world, bringing personal stories to a global audience. Commonwealth Writers believes in the transformative power of creative expression in all its forms. Both responsive and proactive, it works with local and international partners to identify and deliver a wide range of cultural projects. The activities take place in Commonwealth countries, but Commonwealth Writers' community is global.

The Commonwealth Foundation

The Commonwealth Foundation was established by Heads of Government in support of the idea that the Commonwealth is as much an association of peoples as it is of governments. It is a unique, stand-alone organisation; it is funded by and reports to governments, which have given it a mandate to support civil society. The Foundation is dedicated to advancing people's participation in promoting responsive, effective and accountable governance so that ultimately their quality of life is improved. The Foundation is the Commonwealth's agency for arts and culture.

Introduction

David Dabydeen, Maria del Pilar Kaladeen
and Tina K. Ramnarine

This volume marks the centenary of the end of indentureship in the British Empire. Indentureship was a particular form of contracted labour, which has remained largely absent from public discourses, although it has been an important aspect of complex, global and capitalist economic production systems. It bracketed the period of the Atlantic slave trade and spread African, Chinese, European and Indian populations, among others, across four continents. Its inspiration was an imperial desire for a cheap, agricultural workforce. At the height of the British Empire, indentured labour was used in the production of sugar, cocoa, cotton, rubber and tea. In South and East Africa, indentured labourers were also involved in mining and the creation of railway networks. The British additionally made agreements with the Netherlands and France which meant that these countries were able to recruit and dispatch to their colonies indentured labourers from British India.

In the seventeenth century, white European labourers were taken to both North America and the Caribbean on temporary agreements, termed indentures. In Virginia, prior to slavery, some African indentured labourers also formed part of the bonded workforce. The many abuses of this type of labour are evident in the earliest historical records of the system. Kidnapping and enticement both played a role in securing indentured labourers in Europe, who arrived to uniformly poor conditions and treatment in the Caribbean. Sugar became the favoured product of the Caribbean plantations. However, plantation owners believed that white workers would not suffice in either numbers or cost due to the labour-intensive nature of its manufacture. As a consequence, these labourers and the system that brought them to the Caribbean were replaced by the brutal enslavement of Africans. Following the abolition of the slave trade in 1807, planters in the Caribbean began to consider the possibility that they might revive the system that had served them two centuries earlier. In 1811, almost three decades before Indian indenture began, a mass importation of Chinese labourers was being mooted as a substitute for the enslaved African workforce.[1]

---

1   Parliamentary Papers, 1810–11, vol. 2, pp. 409–12.

Indenture was not slavery, but it consistently featured aspects of that system, and its nineteenth-century incarnation was famously labelled little more than a reinvention of slavery.[2] In its pre- and post-slavery forms, indenture functioned in similar ways. Recruits would agree to labour in a foreign land; they were indebted to whoever had paid for their voyage and, on arrival, were bound to a master until their contract expired. Frequently, at the end of their term, the agreement offered indenturees the provision for either a return passage or a portion of land. Real or perceived violations of the contract meant that such labourers were subjected to legal proceedings. In the case of the Indian indenture system, which resulted in the transportation of more than two million men, women and children, the intimacy between the plantocracy and judiciary habitually prevented anything more substantial for the indentured applicant than a pantomime of justice.

The majority of the work in this anthology was inspired by the period of Indian indenture that took place between 1834 and 1917, which was prompted by the abolition of enslavement and by the apprenticeship system's termination. The term 'Gladstone's coolies' is a misnomer that centres the system of indenture and its inception in the Caribbean at the point when John Gladstone, father of the future Prime Minister William Gladstone, engaged a Calcutta firm to source Indian labourers for two of his estates in Guyana (British Guiana). The first Indian indentured labourers had arrived in Mauritius in 1834, while Gladstone's 'experiment' in Guyana took place in 1838. They came to form by far the largest group of these workers in the British Empire, but it is important to acknowledge the presence of other groups in the nineteenth-century indenture system. In the Caribbean, indentured labourers from Africa, the American south and Madeira had arrived in the region from 1834 onwards. In addition, before its abolition in 1917, indenturees travelled to Australia, Fiji, Malaysia (Malaya), Myanamar (Burma), South Africa and Sri Lanka. Within the Caribbean, while Guyana and Trinidad received the majority of such labourers, places like Belize (British Honduras), Grenada, Jamaica, St Kitts and Nevis and St Vincent all had indentured populations too. In the Caribbean, Mauritius and South Africa, Chinese workers formed part of the indentured workforce and more than 60,000 South Sea Islanders were indentured, many forcibly, to Queensland, Australia.

2   Parliamentary Papers, 1840, vol. 34, Lord John Russell to Governor Light, 15 Feb. 1840, pp. 42–4.

While there is no question that some migrants indentured willingly, there is also no doubt that many left their homes without full knowledge of the length of the journey they were undertaking, or how far they were travelling. Coercion, misrepresentation and even kidnapping were all recorded forms of 'recruitment', and the exploitation of the indentured subject continued from embarkation to plantation. In Jamaica, South Africa and Australia, racially inspired legislation sought to prevent Indians and South Sea Islanders from settling in these countries after their indentures were completed.[3] Official enquiries punctuate the history of this system in the Caribbean, where coordinated plantation uprisings in Guyana provoked formal investigations and ultimately contributed to its termination.[4] Wherever indenture occurred in the British Empire stories of resistance followed. This resistance took many forms, whether it was South Sea Islanders petitioning King Edward VII against forced deportation or what the Indian-Fijian historian Brij Lal has described as a 'non-resistance' movement in Fiji, where workers without recourse to other forms of protest, took their own lives in alarming numbers.

Unremarkably, some of the leading writers of the indentured experience have continued this tradition of resistance by focusing their literary work on issues of identity and belonging, and by wrestling with the desire to challenge colonial and indigenous narratives that record them as historical interlopers in countries to which they do not belong. Pioneers of the literature of the indentured labour diaspora include the Trinidadian-born Nobel Laureate V. S. Naipaul, as well as his father (Seepersad) and brother (Shiva). Moreover, the transnational literary legacy of indentured labourers' descendants is rich and substantial. Authors, such as Farida Karodia and Agnes Sam (South Africa); Khal Torabully, Ananda Devi and Natacha Appanah (Mauritius); Subramani, Raymond Pillai and Satendra Nandan (Fiji), have contributed to a formidable body of work that interrogates, in diverse genres, the legacies of indenture. A significant commitment to ensuring the legacy of those who were minorities in the system

---

3   On Jamaica see Walton Look Lai, *Indentured Labour, Caribbean Sugar: Chinese and Indian Migrants to the British West Indies, 1838–1917* (London and Baltimore, MD: John Hopkins University Press, 1993), p. 83; and on Natal see Hugh Tinker, *A New System of Slavery: the Export of Indian Labour Overseas, 1830–1920*, 2nd edn. (London: Hansib, 1993), p. 273.

4   The shooting dead of indentured workers, in the 1913 uprising on plantation Rose Hall in Guyana, was criticised in India, where nationalists considered the system an example of British disregard for Indian lives.

is also evident. Taking Guyana as an example, novels by Peter Kempadoo (*Guyana Boy*, 1960); Moses Nagamootoo (*Hendree's Cure*, 2001); Jan Lowe Shinebourne (*The Last Ship*, 2015); and Rhyaan Shah (*A Silent Life*, 2005) have memorialised in valuable ways the pre- and post-indenture lives of the South Indian, Chinese and Muslim of that country's indentured communities.[5]

In addition to contributions from established writers, this anthology features work by new writers, who are committed to developing the literary legacy established by the mid twentieth century.[6] As the first international anthology to focus on indentureship and its legacies, this book brings together literature based on indentured histories in, for example, the Chagos Islands, Fiji, Guyana, Liberia, Malaysia, Samoa, St Vincent, Trinidad and Sri Lanka. On the centenary of the abolition of indenture in the British Empire it is a privilege for the editors to present this commemorative volume.

5   South Indians and Muslims formed a small proportion of the total of indentured Indians to Guyana between 1838 and 1917. Similarly, due to the fitful nature of Chinese indenture to the colony, this group was also a minority.

6   The copyright of all contributions to the anthology is held by the authors.

Editors' note on the word 'coolie'

This Telegu word, that once merely denoted a labourer, took on new meaning with the inception of the Indian indenture system. Colonial Caribbean newspapers from the turn of the twentieth century published letters from second- and third-generation Indian-Caribbeans revealing that they took great offence at the term and were fully aware of the transition the word had made from its original definition to becoming a slur based on ideas about 'race' directed at them by other cultural groups. Over a century later it is still used in the same way in many countries that imported bonded labour from India, such as Fiji, Guyana, South Africa and Trinidad.

Despite this word's complex legacy, writers from overseas Indian communities have been involved in a process of 'reclamation' around the world 'coolie' since the 1970s. Guyanese poets from Rajkumari Singh (author of the essay 'I am a Coolie', 1973) to David Dabydeen (author of *Coolie Odyssey*, 1988) have embraced the word as a signifier of a distinct cultural identity. The reclamation movement has inadvertently sparked a growing trend among some historians to employ this term casually without reference to the long-standing arguments against it. Tina K. Ramnarine has noted that the blanket use of the term 'coolie' (often applied pejoratively) has erased the complex histories and identities of those who participated in the indenture system. Moreover, not all of these migrants were 'labourers', although colonial representations fostered such social categorisations. Priests, sepoys, artists and performers were all recorded as participants in the indenture system in the Caribbean. Their presence resulted in high levels of literacy, cultural awareness and socially valued performance practices.

Biographies

Editors

DAVID DABYDEEN is one of the leading creative writers of the Indian indentured experience in the Caribbean. He worked at the University of Warwick's Yesu Persaud Centre for Caribbean Studies for over two decades. An award-winning poet and novelist, he has written extensively on migration, belonging and identity. In addition to his work in the academy, Professor Dabydeen has taken part in a number of programmes for British radio and television. He has served as Guyana's Ambassador and Permanent Delegate to UNESCO and from 2010 to 2015 he was Guyana's Ambassador to China.

MARIA DEL PILAR KALADEEN is an associate fellow at the Institute of Commonwealth Studies, School of Advanced Study, University of London. Her academic work focuses on colonial literature about the indenture system in Guyana and her monograph, 'With Eyes of Wonder': Colonial Writing on Indentured Indians in British Guiana, 1838–1917, is forthcoming with Liverpool University Press. Dr Kaladeen has a strong interest in sharing academic research through public and community engagement. She has designed and led academic projects that involved knowledge exchange activities with London's homeless and badly-housed.

TINA K. RAMNARINE is a musician, anthropologist and global cultural explorer at Royal Holloway University of London. Professor Ramnarine researches performance, politics and arts responses to global challenges. Her publications include the books: *Creating Their Own Space: the Development of an Indian-Caribbean Musical Tradition* (2001); *Ilmatar's Inspirations: Nationalism, Globalization, and the Changing Soundscapes of Finnish Folk Music* (2003); *Beautiful Cosmos: Performance and Belonging in the Caribbean Diaspora* (2007); and the edited volumes *Musical Performance in the Diaspora* (2007) and *Global Perspectives on Orchestras: Collective Creativity and Social Agency* (2017).

Contributors

PATTI-ANNE ALI has written, directed and performed for page, stage and screen for more than twenty years. Writings include: *Ian Ali – Great Nationals of Trinidad and Tobago Series* (2013) and the Cacique (Trinidadian theatrical excellence award) nominated play, *Single-An Act of Love* (2004). Performances include: C. Durang's *Miss Witherspoon* (2007) with Amphibian Stage, Fort Worth Texas, USA, and Merchant/Ivory's feature film *The Mystic Masseur* (2001). Patti has directed multiple times for the Shakespeare in Paradise Festival in the Bahamas, and has won advertising copywriting awards. She is a member of the National Theatre Arts Company of Trinidad and Tobago. *Welcome Inn* (2017) is her most recent play.

GAIUTRA BAHADUR is a Guyanese-American writer. Her book *Coolie Woman: The Odyssey of Indenture* was shortlisted for the Orwell Prize, the British literary award for artful political writing. Her debut fiction, the short story 'The Stained Veil', appears in the Feminist Press collection *Go Home!* A former daily newspaper reporter, she is a critic, essayist and journalist: a contributor to the essay anthologies *Nonstop Metropolis* and *Living on the Edge of the World* and to *The New York Times Book Review, Lapham's Quarterly, The Virginia Quarterly Review, Dissent, The Nation* and *Ms.* magazine, among other publications. She is the recipient of fellowships or residencies for creative nonfiction from the MacDowell Artists Colony, Harvard's W.E.B. Du Bois Research Center, the Rockefeller Foundation's Bellagio Center in Italy, the Barbara Deming Memorial Fund and the New Jersey State Council on the Arts. The lyric essay in this volume is a preview of her current book project, which explores the idea of America through its twentieth-century entanglements with her home country.

SUZANNE BHAGAN is a Trinidadian-born writer and international educator. She studied law (LLB) at the University of Warwick and English literature (BA) at the University of the West Indies. She also taught English in Japan with the JET Programme. She enjoys blogging about meaningful globetrotting and has published travel essays and articles in a variety of outlets including *Caribbean Beat, Matador Network, Savvy Tokyo* and *GoAbroad*.

EDDIE BRUCE-JONES is a legal academic and anthropologist based at Birkbeck College, University of London. His latest research project is a legal-historical and narrative-driven study of indentured South Asians to Jamaica and he is currently teaching a new course on race, law and literature. Author of *Race in the Shadow of Law* (Routledge, 2016), and of numerous articles on race, asylum and state violence, he serves on the UK's Institute of Race Relations board. He is also essays editor for the literary magazine, *The Offing*, based in Los Angeles.

DEIRDRE JONKLAAS CADIRAMEN is a Sri Lankan of Dutch-Burgher heritage, educated in Colombo. Prompted by a stay in India she embarked on creative writing in 2000 and has published three books. She was shortlisted for the 2002 David T K Wong Fellowship, one of her stories was translated into Telugu for an anthology of Sri Lankan Women's short fiction, and her Austin A35 restoration story won second prize in the July 2008 issue of the UK-based *Classic Cars* magazine. Her childhood on Ceylon tea and rubber plantations gave her a first-hand insight into indentured labour.

STELLA CHONG SING is an educator and emerging writer from Port-of-Spain, Trinidad and Tobago. Her research interests include existential literature, postcolonial literature, feminist studies, and Indian-Caribbean history and identity. She currently teaches communication studies and English language and literature in Trinidad and Tobago. Some of her poems were included in Brock University's literary anthology, *Looking for Trees: A Brock University Anthology of Creative Writing* (2009). Stella dedicates her time to working with underserved young people in a Port-of-Spain community-based project.

GITAN DJELI (Gitanjali Pyndiah's pen name for non-fiction and poetry) is a London-based Mauritian writer and researcher in cultural studies at Goldsmiths, University of London. She is interested in decolonial historiographies and creative practices (art, literature and music in Creole mothertongues). Her latest publications (2018) are: an encyclopedia entry, 'Malcolm de Chazal: Surrealism in the Indian Ocean' (Bloomsbury Academic); the article 'Sonic landscape of seggae: Mauritian sega meets Jamaican roots reggae' (Intellect Books); and the book chapter 'Performative historiography of the mothertongue: reading "kreol" outside a colonial and nationalist approach' (The University of Mauritius Press).

PRITHIRAJ DULLAY was born in 1946 in Port Shepstone, Kwa-Zulu Natal, South Africa. An active opposer of Apartheid fascism, he was exiled in Denmark for fourteen years. Still an activist, he remains fully committed to constitutional democracy. Prithiraj has lectured at universities in Denmark and South Africa. The author of *Salt Water Runs in My Veins* (2010) and nearly 200 columns published globally, he has been featured in *Connecting the Dots* ed. B. Mathew (Kerala,

2017) and *Vintage Indian South African Writings* ed. R. Chetty (STE, Cape Town, 2010). His new book *How Europe Ravaged the World* is due shortly. Contact: exilewriting@gmail.com.

PRIYA N. HEIN is the author of several popular children's books published in English, French, Creole and German. For several years, she wrote a monthly feature for a British newspaper. Her books have been recommended by, inter alia, l'Alliance Française, *l'Express*, Fédération Nationale d'Achats des Cadres, *Süddeutsche* newspaper and the Pill Mayer Intercultural Foundation. The Mauritius Institute of Education and Ludwig-Maximilians University, Munich, have selected her books to use as teaching materials. She has been invited to participate in numerous book fairs and programmes for Mauritian radio and television, and was shortlisted for the Outstanding Young Person's Award, Mauritian Achievers Award and nominated for the Astrid Lindgren Memorial Award.

GABRIELLE JAMELA HOSEIN is an Indian-Caribbean feminist poet, writer, scholar and activist. She has been involved in feminist movement-building for more than twenty years and is currently head of the Institute for Gender and Development Studies, University of the West Indies, St Augustine campus. Her publications include: 'No pure place for resistance: reflections on being Ms. Mastana Bahar' (in *Bindi*, 2011); 'Modern navigations: Indo-Trinidadian girlhood and gender differential creolisation (*CRGS*, 2012), and 'Democracy, gender and Indian Muslim modernity in Trinidad', in *Islam and the Americas* (2015). She is co-editor of the anthology, *Indo-Caribbean Feminist Thought: Genealogies, Theories, Enactments* (2016), and her blog, 'Diary of a Mothering Worker', is published weekly in the Trinidad *Guardian* newspaper.

KEVIN JARED HOSEIN is an award-winning writer from Trinidad and Tobago. He has published two books: *The Repenters* (currently nominated for the 2018 International Dublin Literary Award) and *Littletown Secrets*. His writings have been published in numerous anthologies and outlets including *Lightspeed Magazine* and *adda*. His other accolades include the 2015 Commonwealth Short Story Prize (Caribbean winner) and the Burt Award for Caribbean Literature, for his novel manuscript *The Beast of Kukuyo* (to be published in 2018).

FAWZIA MURADALI KANE is an architect and poet. Born in Trinidad and Tobago, she came to the UK on a scholarship to study architecture, and is now a director of KMK Architects in London. Her poetry has been extensively published in journals including *Poetry Review* and *Poetry London*. Her poem 'Kaieteur Falls' was shortlisted for the 2017

Montreal International Poetry Prize. Her debut poetry collection *Tantie Diablesse* (2011) was longlisted in the 2012 Bocas Lit Fest prize, and Thamesis has published her long sequence *Houses of the Dead* (2014). She is now working on a novel, *La Bonita Cuentista.*

CYNTHIA KISTASAMY. A graduate in fine arts from the University of Durban-Westville in 1999, Cynthia is now a fine artist living in Johannesburg, South Africa. She has worked for the Department of Arts and Culture (2001–6), in museums across KwaZulu-Natal, South Africa. Her writing career began two years ago and she has won accolades for the short-story piece, 'The Storm Walkers' (*Expound* magazine, 9, 2017); the short story 'Shiva Eyes', which was long-listed for the Short. Sharp. Stories Award at the National Arts Festival (2017); and 'Pepsi, Pie and Swimming Pools-in-the Sky' (included in this anthology), which was listed in the results of the SA Writer's College Short Story Award (2017) under 'Stories we loved'.

BRIJ V. LAL, Fiji-born grandson of a girmitiya, taught history at the universities of the South Pacific (Suva), Hawaii at Manoa (Honolulu) and, for twenty-five years, at the Australian National University where he is now an emeritus professor. He is widely regarded as one of the leading historians of the Indian indentured diaspora. His many books include: *Girmitiyas: The Origins of the Fiji Indians* (1983); *Broken Waves: A History of the Fiji Islands in the 20th Century* (1992); *Chalo Jahaji: On a Journey Through Indenture in Fiji* (2000) and *Mr Tulsi's Store: A Fijian Journey'* (2001), which the San Francisco-based Kiriyama Prize judged to be one of the 'Ten notable books of Asia-Pacific' in 2002. His many awards include Australia's Centenary of Federation Medal for his contribution to the humanities there, a fellowship at the Australian Humanities Academy, and a Member of the Order of Australia in 2015 for his contribution to Pacific scholarship. He was honoured with a festschrift, 'Bearing Witness', in 2017.

KAMA LA MACKEREL is a performer, writer, storyteller, community-arts facilitator and multidisciplinary artist whose work explores aesthetic practices for marginalised communities to adopt as forms of resilience and resistance. Using performance, poetry, textiles, installations, screen-printing and digital arts, Kama's work is both deeply personal and political, articulating an anti-colonial praxis through cultural production. Kama has performed, exhibited and run community arts programmes internationally, including in Toronto, Vancouver, New York, Boston, Paris, London, Amsterdam, Berlin and Pune. Kama was born in Mauritius, immigrated to India as a young adult, and now lives in Montréal, Canada. More information: *lamackerel.net*.

LELAWATTEE MANOO-RAHMING is an Indian-Caribbean poet, fiction writer, artist, essayist and a professional mechanical/building services engineer. A prize-winning author, her writing focuses on violence against women and children, the environment and her Indo-Trinidadian heritage. Her work has appeared in numerous journals and anthologies including *WomanSpeak; The Caribbean Writer; Poui;* and *Interviewing the Caribbean*. She is the author of *Curry Flavour* (Peepal Tree Press, 2000); and *Immortelle and Bhandaaraa Poems* (Proverse Hong Kong, 2011). She is a dual citizen of Trinidad and Tobago, where she was born and grew up, and the Bahamas, where she resides and practises engineering.

NOELLE NIVE MOA, a mother of five, is a New Zealand-born Samoan, self-taught artist, printmaker and bookbinder. Her writing and poetry has appeared in *Niu Voices: Contemporary Pacific Fiction I* (2006), *JAAM* 29 (2011), *Blackmail Press* poetry ezine, 24 and 42. She has written two books and several short stories that explore Pacific colonialism, diaspora, loss and belonging. These works have enjoyed continued popularity at the bottom of rather large shabby-chic boxes in the corner of her room. Maybe one day she will be brave enough to submit them, but for now she's busy trying to find new hiding places to keep her stash of Russian fudge away from her annoyingly clever tribe of children.

AKHTAR MOHAMMED was born in Vancouver, Canada, to Fijian Muslim parents of Indian descent. He obtained a BA in political science from the University of British Columbia, an LLB at SOAS, University of London, and recently completed an LLM at Osgoode Hall Law School in Toronto. In 2013 he became the founding president and chairman of the board of governors of SOAS's Islamic Finance and Ethics Society, later expanding the society to a number of London universities. Akhtar is also the author of the upcoming *What Is Islamic Finance and Why Should We Care?* (Garnet Publishing, 2018).

SATENDRA NANDAN was born in Fiji and studied in Delhi, Leeds and Canberra. His collected volume of poems, *The Loneliness of Islands*, was published in 2007, and his fifth volume of poetry, *Across the Seven Seas*, came out in March 2017 to mark the centenary of the abolition of Indian indenture, 1917–2017. Satendra is currently completing his sixth poetry volume, *Gandhianjali*, to be published on 15 May 2018, Girmit Day in Fiji. He's also writing a novel as a visiting fellow at the Humanities Research Centre, Australian National University. Now an emeritus professor and a member of the world's first International Institute of Poetry Studies at the University of Canberra, Satendra Nandan was elected to the Fijian Parliament in 1982 and 1987. He was Fiji's first Labour MP and a cabinet minister in Dr Timoci Bavadra's coalition government in 1987. He was appointed to the Fiji Constitution Commission in 2012. Email: Satendra.Nandan@gmail. com.

ANGELICA A. OLUOCH is a student, currently pursuing a degree in linguistics and English literature, in Kenya. She has just begun to explore the literary sphere, and seeks to share with the world, through the stories she tells, her experiences growing up and living in 'New' Africa. Some of her fiction is due to be published in literary journals, and she has been featured in 'Fifty-Word Stories'. Angelica also mentors young people with a budding interest in creative writing.

JENNIFER RAHIM is Trinidadian. She is a widely published poet, fiction writer and literary critic. Her poetry collection, *Approaching Sabbaths* (2009), was awarded a Casa de las Américas Prize in 2010. Her other poetry collections include *Redemption Rain: Poems* (2011) and *Ground Level: Poems* (2014). *Songster and Other Stories* appeared in 2007 and *Curfew Chronicles: A Fiction* in 2017. She also edited and introduced *Beyond Borders: Cross Culturalism and the Caribbean Canon* (2009) and *Created in the West Indies: Caribbean Perspectives on V.S. Naipaul* (2011) with Barbara Lalla. Her new collection of poems, *Homing Now to Stardust*, will soon be released.

MARY ROKONADRAVU is a Fijian writer. She ran a prison-writing programme in seven correctional facilities in Fiji's capital, Suva, for four years, and edited the Pacific's first anthology of prison writing, *Shedding Silences*, in 2008. She won the 2015 Regional Commonwealth Short Story Prize (Pacific) and was shortlisted in 2017. Her dream is to contribute to the growth of the vibrant Pacific islands writing and publishing sector – and to Pacific islanders reading and valuing their own stories and voices. She will be teaching a creative writing course at the University of the South Pacific in 2018. Twitter: @rokonadravu2.

ANITA SETHI is an award-winning journalist, writer and critic who has written for many publications including *The Guardian* and *Observer, Sunday Times, Telegraph, FT Life & Arts, Independent, i paper, Times Literary Supplement, Granta* and *New Statesman*, and has appeared on BBC radio. Her writing has been published in several anthologies and she is currently completing a book. Website: www.anitasethi. co.uk. Twitter: @anitasethi. Instagram: @anitasethi.

ANIROOD SINGH is a High Court advocate, counsellor-at-law, a published writer of fiction and non-fiction and a professional editor. *The Diary of Henry Francis Fynn: Meeting Shaka* was published in 2015, and *Municipal Representation as a Mechanism for Efficient Service Delivery in South Africa* is scheduled for publication in 2018. Anirood is a director of Warpath Records and Orocci Pictures. He is a member of the International Bar Association, PEN, Academic and Non-Fiction Authors Association, Writers Guild, SA Translators' Institute, SA Freelancers' Association and the Professional Editors' Guild.

ANEETA SUNDARARAJ trained as a lawyer in the UK and practised in Malaysia before she decided to pursue her dream of writing. Since publishing her first novel in 2003, she has worked on several non-fiction works that include books on independent financial services, psychiatry, cardiology and Ayurveda. Her writing has also appeared in magazines, ezines and journals together with more than 280 feature articles published in Malaysia's *New Straits Times*. For more than a decade she has been maintaining the 'How to Tell a Great Story' website, a resource for storytellers, which she created and developed at www.howtotellagreatstory.com. 'The Legend of *Nagakanna*' is a chapter in her as-yet-unpublished novel, *The Age of Smiling Secrets*.

ARNOLD THOMAS is a retired diplomat from the Organization of Eastern Caribbean States Embassy in Brussels. He was previously professor of political science at Brooklyn College, New York, and lecturer in Caribbean history at Thames Valley University, London. He also spent several years at the CARICOM Secretariat in Guyana as chief of the technical assistance section. He is a founding member of the St Vincent and the Grenadines (SVG) Indian Heritage Foundation, a life member of the Global Organization of People of Indian Origin, SVG coordinator of the International Indian Diaspora Council, and member of the SVG UNESCO Committee on International Memory of the World Programme.

ATHOL WILLIAMS is an award-winning South African poet and social philosopher. He has published four collections of poetry, had poems published in forty literary publications and received four poetry awards – Sol Plaatje EU Poetry Award for 2015 and 2016, 2016 Parallel Universe Poetry Prize at Oxford University, and the 2017 South African Independent Publishers Award for Poetry. Athol's autobiography, *Pushing Boulders: Oppressed to Inspired*, chronicles his escape from Apartheid. He holds degrees from Oxford, Harvard, London School of Economics, Massachusetts Institute of Technology,

London Business School and Witwatersrand (Wits) University. His creative and scholarly work focuses on advancing structural social justice and ethical development.

The Rebel

Kevin Jared Hosein

Varin wake me up to ask me if I want to go see a dead man.

My lil brother Bansi was sleepin next to me. Ma was making we wear beadstrings cause she say it have a woman in another barracks put a spirit lash on Bansi. The boy was burnin up. Papa say if he have to dead he rather he dead here where he was borned.

The last time we went to the clinic was when my lil sister Ushi had the stomach sickness and was shittin water. Have a bridge all of we use to go down where the swampwater meet the river, where it have real plenty mulletfish. We put a piece of roti on a needle and dip it in the water. If you see how the fish was coming up! But Ushi so stupid she gon and drinkin the water just so she could spit it in all of we face. And the stupid girl was laughin hard-hard while she doin it.

When she get sick we laugh and say it was good for she. Papa had to beg somebody to take she to the clinic but he say when they reach, the negra woman take too long to get the doctor and Ushi did dead right there on the floor. Me and Bansi get licks that night cause Papa feel it was we who tell she to drink the water.

They burn Ushi down by the Caroni River. And nearly everybody in the barracks get sick. Nobody else did dead though. Mister Ward come down mad like the devil when he find out why everybody get sick. So he take away Papa coolie pass for a week and we get licks again that night.

I tell Varin to gon sleep cause I ent gettin up to see no dead body. I tell him I see plenty already. But he was shakin me still and asking if I ever see one without the head.

I tell him he lyin.

No no, he say. He say he gon show me it. He tell me I have to come quick before dog and bird find it.

So I get up from the bed and put on my pants and follow Varin. We make sure to be real quiet. I tell Varin if he was tryin to get me in

1

trouble I was gon catch a spider and put it in he pillow. He laugh and tell me he ent fraid spider.

It was dark outside. The rain was fallin whole evening and the river was floodin a lil bit. The water was thick like dal. The sky was black black but the moon was showin through the clouds. But I still couldnt see where I was goin.

You blind, Varin tell me.

I didnt say nothin cause I know people use to be seein things in the night that I couldnt see. Like had a time a scorpion come in the room and Ma was bawlin like a jackass. She hand me a broom and was tellin me kill it kill it! And my eye goin all over the place and the floor was just black. She was making so much noise that the scorpion end up stingin she in she ankle. If she wasnt bawlin like how she was bawlin the scorpion woulda pass she straight! She fall down like God knock she down. The other children was laughing like mad. When Papa come home and hear what happen he take out the rattan for me.

I follow Varin right into the canefield. Where we was walkin, the water was gettin past we ankle. I tell him it does have snake in the water. He laugh and say he ent fraid snake.

Look it there, he say. He run to it. I couldnt see nothin. I went closer and still couldnt see nothin. I know the body was there cause I coulda hear the flies.

I ask Varin to point at it.

He laugh and ask me if I blind.

I tell him just point at it. And he point at it.

I went closer and then I see it. I see the head before I see the body. Varin hold up the head to show me. Was boss man O'Bannon. I remember thunder roll the same time Varin pick up the man head. God was mad. Put it down boy, I tell Varin. So he throw it next to the body. I was never so frighten in all my life. I didnt even feel so when Ushi was sick and dead.

You see the neck? Varin ask me. He ask if I ent find the colour look like when they cut up goat. He was laughing when he was sayin it. How he was laughing I was wonderin at the time if it was he self who chop off the man head. I couldnt see but I ent say nothin cause all he woulda tell me was how I blind.

2

I ask Varin who he think do it. Then he tell me he see who do it. He see it when it happen in the late evenin with he own two big eye.

Is Salaman who do it, he say.

Salaman use to live with we in the barracks. But he save up enough to buy a house and land a few months back. I ent know how old he was. Maybe fifty. Probably a lil older. All I know is he was here before any of we. He was old like stone but still he went and marry Tanvi who did now turn seventeen. Salaman wasnt he real name though. Is Salaman he use to call heself but everybody know it had somethin funny bout him. He had a blade he keep in he room. Wasnt no cutlass or grassknife. Was a slick piece of iron look like it coulda lop off bison head in one slice. He never use to talk so much but when he talk, you know he wasnt the same as the rest of we.

He had beard like wire and a scar on he neck that look like a butterfly. He skin – people say it look black, but to me it look gray. Like smoke. He eyes was like a white man own. A boy in the barracks, Lalit, have them same kinda eyes. Lalit mother say is cause she have Kashmir blood in she that Lalit come out so. But everybody know Lalit father is either a overseer or a overseer son.

Salaman had the money to buy house and land cause I never see him drinkin rum. Not like Papa and them who does go smoke and drink by the chinee man shop everytime they get pay. He always comin home lookin like he get dredge outta the river. You have to make sure everything clean-clean when he come home or else he gon put you to stand up in the barrel and leave you there. One time he put Bansi in the barrel cause he spill goatmilk on heself. Bansi have bendfoot so he was cryin and bawlin the whole time.

Salaman come in the room a day and tell Papa he tryin to sleep and how to shut that child up. Papa was movin to beat Bansi but Salaman say that would only make the boy cry more. Papa get vex-vex after and look to knock down Salaman. But Salaman put the man on the floor with one cuff. He then lift Bansi out of the barrel and put him on the bed.

The next week Salaman buy a bottle of rum and bring it for Papa. They sit down on the ground and was takin sips out of the bottle. I was on the bed pretendin to sleep. Salaman get drunk easy. That was when he tell Papa bout when he was back in India and how he kill a few white man up in Lucknow right before he come on the boat to Trinidad. He say he was a rebel. Say they use to call him *sepoy*. Papa ask him why he kill the white man and he say is because they force

3

him to eat cowfat – that how when he had to load gun, they make him bite the casing for the bullet and it had cowfat in it. The white man was godless and that he was a man of God.

Papa laugh. Salaman tell him that all of we here in the barracks was animals and he dunno how we happy to live so. This was right before he buy the house and land. Papa laugh again. He probably forget the whole story by now. He make sure to drink out the rum before anybody else ask for it.

Varin was moving up he hand when he was tellin me how Salaman had O'Bannon on the ground and was choppin choppin at he neck. I tell him we have to get outta here before Salaman come back. I feel like I coulda barely move. I was movin my toes and feelin for snake the whole time. Varin ask me who we feel we should tell. I tell him not to tell nobody. Let the bird and them tell them. Not we.

So we walk back to the barracks. The rain come down as soon as we reach back. Everybody was still sleepin. I sleep for a lil bit but I keep waking up. I keep seeing the head.

In the mornin everybody was all over the place. A white man come to we on a horse and tell we hellfire comin for all of we coolie. I feel he was goin barracks to barracks sayin that. I look at Varin. I thought he was gon say something but he didnt. Mister Ward come round to the barracks later a lil while after asking who was where yesterday evenin. When he was done doin that, he look at Tara. He tell she how she daughter dead. How they find the body in Salaman bedroom with the head cut off.

As soon as he say that Tara start to bawl. She sound like how chicken does sound when you readying the knife. Tara was Tanvi mother. Tara never like Salaman except when he buy house and come back and say he wanted to put Tanvi in it. She was always sayin he was too black and people might think Tanvi gon and marry a negro. Tanvi was pretty and lightskin and ripe. Salaman was always saying how she always look so clean and pure. When Tanvi marry Salaman we never really see she again. Tara use to go over to the house but she coulda never stay long. Whenever she come back she say Tanvi was happy.

Had a boy name Bikram. All of we use to watch Tanvi when she bathe. Had a slit in the galvanize[1] where you coulda peep through.

---

1   Corrugated metal structure.

We see all the woman and them. Even old woman Pimmi who was fat like ox and had big nasty bush covering all she choot. I remember I cuff down Bikram and Varin cause I catch them watchin Ma.

Tanvi did like how we use to watch. She use to poke out she tongue at we. But when she did marry and gone we couldnt do that again. Bikram was the only one who was mad bout that. So had a day he went to Salaman house early in the mornin to see if he coulda catch a peep. We tell him it didnt make no sense cause Salaman house had proper wall and fence. He say he was still goin. When he come back we ask him what he see. He ent say nothin. He was quiet for the rest of the day. But he use to still go and watch. I wasnt goin nowhere by Salaman property. Not after seein how he knock down Papa like he hand was a bullhorn.

Tara start runnin through the floodwater. She look like a big horse how she was moving. Some of the big men follow. Papa was one. Varin and me went too. Run a whole mile down the road till we get to the house. But it was block off. Officers was there already. Get these coolies outta here, they say.

Tara start cussin and beatin up she body like a rooster. The officer take he baton and hit she one hard lash in she hip and then punch the side of she head.

Where Salaman? Papa ask the officer. He was bracing for the lash. Tell we where Salaman is and we go deal wit him!

The officer say they ent need no help from no coolie and to go back to the barracks. When we went back Ma and some of the women wipe up the blood from Tara face. Isha bring milk for she and Uma bring rum. I remember hearin Brudder Dilip askin why Tara have to get on like a ass, how she have three other daughter to mind.

Bikram come to ask me if I see the body. I tell him how the place was block off. He look quiet like he did know something. He tell me to follow him by the bison pond. So I went. Then he start tellin me a story bout how he see O'Bannon in Salaman house the time he went to peep. He say O'Bannon was lyin down on top of Tanvi and he move up he hands to show me what they was doin. I tell him how that is a normal thing. He shake he head and try to tell me I lyin. Then I tell him that was how Lalit was borned.

Bikram look down at the ground like he dog now dead. He say he ent know that is a normal thing. I tell him yea – how O'Bannon house had like a hundred window and nobody couldnt tell nothin to somebody like that. I ask him how Tanvi did look when he see she with O'Bannon. He say she look like she was sleepin. Bikram say he think Salaman kill she and he was gon kill Salaman. But I know he wasnt gon do nothin. Bikram ask me what I know bout Salaman. Bikram is a cry cry baby who you mustnt tell nothin to. So I ent say nothin.

Was a good thing too because later that evenin Bikram went and tell he mother everything he tell me. And she went and tell the whole barracks. Officers still wasnt lettin nobody see the body or go in the house. So they set up some cards and rum in the barracks that night. Everybody was sittin and crowdin the front.

Ma say, Even if that whole thing happen, he ent have to cut off she head.

Brudder Dilip say, The girl use to carry sheself like a bitch in heat. Man like O'Bannon dont just ups so and do them kinda thing.

Isha say, She probably make the mistake of tellin Salaman what happen. If that happen to me I ent tellin my husband notten!

Brudder Dilip then say, Man does find out!

Uma say, Why you dont gon find Salaman now eh?

Papa say, Had to have something happen before O'Bannon lie down on she. That was when she shoulda tell Salaman what was goin on. Either she did like it or she was too stupid to tell.

Ma say, She was too young to tell thing like that, boy.

Brudder Dilip say, The bitch well know how to drive man mad.

Tara was quiet the whole time. I went back inside after bout an hour. Bansi was feelin a lil better. He ask me to ask Ma to make some tea for him. But I make it myself. Ma say Tara ent say nothin the whole night – how she was frighten the woman was goin mad. But Tara bawl out the whole night while everybody was sleepin.

Bout two days later they arrest Salaman on the port. He was hiding on a ship goin back to India. They lock he up in the jail. This was what Mister Ward tell we. He say that Salaman write a letter to the Guvnah and the Guvnah actually went to see him. I dunno if anything else happen after that. Mister Ward tell everybody that the best thing to do was stop talkin bout it and to just get back to work.

We had to wait a while to get back Tanvi body. They say it was all mix up and was gon take a while to fix she up. They put a wood dowel in she neck to connect the head back to the body. Mister Ward say they would burn the body in the city. He could only afford for Tara and she daughters to go. He pay for the carriage and all.

I remember how everybody suck their teeth for that. Papa and Brudder Dilip was the loudest. Papa bawl out, My child dead and you take way my coolie pass, but she child dead and she gettin carriage ride?

Mister Ward tell him to shut he damn mouth and how he was only doing this cause nobody in the barracks couldnt afford to dirty up the river for everybody to get sick again. He say he could exchange all of we for a steampower tractor and leave we to starve and dead. Everybody shut up after that.

Tara had a big big smile on she face as she went in the carriage. If you see she!

The sun was out bright on that day. All the picoplat and kiskadee[2] come out to sing. Mister Ward give everybody their tasks and tell we that a new overseer was comin today. He tell we to be on we best conduct and to pray and ask God that this one turn out to be a good man too.

*

---

2   Two species of bird.

Mother Wounds

Gitan Djeli

Brought up for half of my pre-adult years by my mother, I have often wondered about the woman who mothered her. My mother does not remember her. Nobody seems to know much about her. I sometimes see my mother's past as a page, made blank by the click of a delete button.

We had no photo albums. I remember witnessing my mother's sisters and brothers together when their father was on his death bed. Only a faded ghostly photograph, which I later saw at the house of one of my aunts, was a reminder of my grandmother's existence. I lived in the silence of her absence for most of my life.

In my more mature years, I became interested in the notion of the mother wound, which is the generational trauma carried by women and passed down to their daughters and granddaughters in a patriarchal society, especially in relation to the inherent domestic violence within my close and extended family. I became fixated on my matrilineage and on the lives of the many mothers who came before me. The stories, which I retrieved from family members and from years of enquiries climbing up the family tree, in parallel with my PhD research entitled *Decolonial Aesthesis and Autopoesis*, brought me to the first woman who left India for Mauritius (during the English indenture period), and birthed the consequent mothers who would eventually bring me to existence.

Here is the story of my journey.

One day at a family gathering, I was approached by a kind-looking old man, whom I had never met before. He was presumably my mother's uncle, my grandmother's brother. I remember vividly how his plain-spoken reflection would set me on a trail of existential questions. The words, which he blurted out with incredible tenderness and allurement, were: 'You look so much like Gouna!'

Gouna[1]

I was surprised. Yet, her name was vaguely familiar. The framed black-and-white portrait of her in my aunt's living room was, at that point, a blurred image in my memory and her name resonated feebly. I figured out that the physiognomy of a petite, South Indian-looking girl in that photograph bore a close resemblance to my own appearance, especially since the skin tones and corpulence of the women in my family ranged from the very fair, tall and round to the very dark and petite. That I, in my early twenties, was being made aware that I looked like my maternal grandmother was a revelation I felt was probably overdue. Her name – Gouna Damayantee Pyndiah – would become an integral part of me. I knew then that I was destined to carry the same initials and surname. Although the faded monochromatic photograph was vocal in its spectrality, it was the first time I had heard someone speak of her as if she had existed as a real person. My mother's uncle affectionately portrayed her as sensitive and resilient. Gouna was, after all, his eldest sister who passed away before she was thirty, a few days after giving birth to her eighth child (not including the miscarriages). She could barely breastfeed and take care of my mother, the seventh born, due to exhaustion and the undiagnosed chronic illness that accompanied most of her pregnancies.

I would spend years collecting photographs from my large extended family and I was able to build a mental picture of Gouna. In a photograph from the late 1940s, sent to me by my uncle (the oldest sibling who still had strong embodied memories of his mother), my grandmother is in her early twenties and wearing an exquisite saree, with an ornate brooch on her right shoulder holding the pleats of her blouse tight. She wears a thick necklace – the stiff ring round her neck holds a big medallion perfectly in place in her notch – and a large, elegant nose stud. Her head is slightly tilted to the left, her eyes are alert and her eyebrows cast a deep shadow on her face. Her dark hair seems to be tied in a bun, with a casual curly strand of hair on her forehead. Although gazing firmly at the camera, she seems reluctant or dispassionate. Her smile is forced, restrained and blank. I sense that an eerie grey silence surrounds her and she looks stoically sad. In a studio family photograph where she is probably seven or eight years old, Gouna stands clumsily, slightly apart from the others,

---

1   The closest translation of the word Gouna, गुण, *guṇá*, in the English language would be 'quality'.

her arms slack and falling lazily across her small frame. She looks very unassuming, her presence lost amidst her brothers and sisters. Her thin legs and wobbly knees almost touching each other seem to evoke a certain physical fragility. Her shoulder-length curly hair looks lifeless. In quite a sinister way, her eyes seem to move outside their sockets as she stares hard, in a downwards glance. She looks completely detached as if her body is not present. She focuses almost blankly as if she has been staring at a dot on the concrete studio floor for several minutes.

An encounter which allowed me to imagine what my grandmother's life had been like was a conversation I had with her much younger sister, who was born at almost the same time as Gouna's first child. It was not rare for mother and daughter to be impregnated at the same time, as women would sometimes give birth to their twelfth or fifteenth child as their first was doomed to motherhood around the age of fourteen. I spent a considerable amount of time conversing with Gouna's sister, who herself had two children at the time. She remembers Gouna as having had a painful existence, full of distress. She recalls the day-long bus journey she undertook with her mother to visit her sister in Goodlands, a village in the extreme north of the island. Gouna had moved there after an arranged marriage her mother deeply regretted. Gouna's mistreatment left an indelible mark on both younger sister and mother. The former recounted an episode where Gouna, heavily pregnant and in excruciating pain, was sent to collect water from the well and was orally abused, by the mother-in-law, for 'procrastinating' instead of carrying out her household chores. She apparently blurted out that Gouna was a 'good for nothing' who deserved to die.

I would read about her extreme strength and tenacity as a mother and wife, married to someone who, with the complicity of his family, kept hidden a relationship with a Creole woman with whom he had a daughter.[2] Highly educated for her time and gender, Gouna spent a decade devoid of intellectual and artistic activities after leaving her family. Through many of her subsequent pregnancies, she was apparently unsupported and suffered from dangerous fevers. This was the reality, in the early twentieth century, for many women of Indian origin in Mauritius. Domestic violence is still a great concern today within my own family and across the country. I've always had the sense that the hierarchies of the plantation were internalised in the

---

2   From Loga Virahsawmy, *The Lotus Flower: a conversation with Dev Virahsawmy* (Mauritius: Caractère Ltee, 2017), pp. 14–15.

private sphere with the mother-in-law acting out the power denied to her as a woman and, in that context, perpetuating patriarchal violence.

Gouna's body collapsed less than a week after the eighth birth. Nobody I spoke to seemed to know the medical reason for her death. 'She died exhausted of child-bearing' seemed to be the answer that most of them believed. The children were dispersed and brought up by the extended family, grandparents and aunts, and the husband's household probably soon forgot Gouna to make space for the everyday management of so many young children. The patriarch, Gouna's father-in-law, later bought a colonial house in town for this purpose. He was a *sirdar* (supervisor) who had acquired wealth and bought land. The motherless children received a privileged education, conferred on them by an ascendant new bourgeoisie in the colony. This in many ways explains why many of Gouna's children were so disconnected from the tormented life of their deceased mother. The patriarchal colony was after all about the survival of the fittest worker, and women who were brought to the colony to 'settle men' during indenture, became isolated from their usual reliable communities of familial care. In the drive to climb the social ladder, and to become respectable according to colonial norms, any mental or physical vulnerabilities or fragilities of body were despised and silenced.

Gouna's own mother was particularly distressed and angry about the fate of her first daughter. She had herself experienced three marriages and had eventually settled into the typical domestic life combining motherhood with manic work supervised by her mother-in-law. She did, however, become known as someone who was ferociously demanding and selective when it came to the marriages of her other daughters. I can only imagine how the pain of Gouna's death must have urged her to empower her other daughters by imposing certain strict criteria for the selection and approval of future suitors. Marriage in the colony represented the union of different families from often-similar linguistic practices, here Telegou, and the solidification of their traditions in the colony. Marriage was also a means of social mobility and a 'good' one would minimise the precarity of a daughter's life, as there were not many ways in which women could acquire independence and safety in the plantation colony. It was only in the mid 1930s that Mauritian society was transformed by a rising workers' consciousness and the nationalist movement of decolonisation. In the midst of political movement and resistance in the early 1950s, Gouna's youngest sister resisted the predetermined path imposed on women and followed her passion for the arts.

It is interesting to note how the village where Gouna grew up, Quartier Militaire, in the heart of the island on the periphery of sugar-cane plantations and with a mixed population of Creoles, Indians and Chinese, was a dynamic creative space. Here, Malagasy, African and Asian musical, artistic and performing traditions merged into diasporic genres. I would become familiar with Geet-Gawai, a Bhojpuri pre-wedding ritual and song-and-dance tradition, which had been brought by North Indians and was performed in certain areas of Quartier Militaire and the surrounding villages. Through rituals reinforcing community identity and cultural memory, practical life knowledges were transmitted by older women through visceral expressions. One of the encounters that impressed me most in my adolescent years was when I witnessed this performance. The powerful experience of watching quite old women playing the *dholak* (a two-headed drum) displaying considerable stamina, and seeing them sing and dance for hours through the night – lifting their sarees as they moved vigorously to the beat – remains ingrained in me. The rural areas where Indians built sustainable communities outside the hierarchies of the plantation economy were crucial spaces where knowledges from both the African and Asian continents – medicinal, spiritual, educational, leadership – were preserved, and where the movements for independence against an alien European exploitative culture emerged.

Gouna's home seems to have embraced the rural Creoleness which informs most of the countryside where Creole is spoken. An Africanised language of communication, it was developed by enslaved Africans during the eighteenth century's French system of slavery in the Indian Ocean region, and adapted by Indians who were recruited to work on the sugar plantations after the abolition of slavery. I would find out that Tifrer, a *sega*[3] artist acclaimed in the 1960s, held the family in high esteem.[4] He was a *zanfan lakaz* (child of the house), a person who is not blood-related but considered to be a close family member, who used to play the *sega* at Gouna's home on the morning of New Year's day. It is also highly possible that Tifrer, meaning 'little brother', was a nickname given to him by the family. Whether the women of the family questioned the lyrics of

3   A polymorphous performative art form in the Creole language comprising songs, dance and specific musical instruments like the *ravann*.

4   Boum Pyndiah: personal audio featuring Tifrer made in 1978.

some of his songs, which are stereotypical and often sexist residues of coloniality, remains to be discovered.

I describe Gouna's mother's home as such because of her long stays there (before her ultimate demise) to recover from illness during a decade of married life and continuous pregnancies. Gouna's tragic fate is a story embedded in the pain, trauma and violence of having motherhood imposed by the marriage system on a body solely utilised to produce expendable labour for the colony, and without contraceptive knowledge being transmitted from grandmother to mother. I want to remember her as a creative soul at heart, an impression formed from reading her eldest child's poetic tribute to her. That child would become the first Creole language activist on the island. She is well remembered for singing mostly in Creole, despite the taboo around the language.

Lavwa Gouna, mo mama,	Gouna's voice, my mum's,
Ankor sant dan mo disan	Still sings in my blood
Kiltir Quartier Militaire	Quartier Militaire's culture
Kan Ti-frer alim dife	When Tifrer lit the fire
Pou sof sawal ravane,	To warm up ravanne's rhythm
Pou triyang so prop kadans,	And tingle through beats and bumps
Amenn kiltir popiler	People's culture
Dan sato Samazeste.	Into the castle.
Lavwa Gouna, mo mama,	Gouna's voice, my mum's,
Dan lapousier Foukalend	In Crazylands dust
Kontinie fer mwa rapel	Still reminds me
Lagam enn sante fezer	Of a rare decadence
Ki ti ne dan lamizer	Born in pain
Pou pran plas dan diksioner.	And now mainstream.[5]

It was as a result of my research on Gouna that tracing my matrilineage became a project of extreme urgency for me. How could I bring visibility to the women who mothered the mothers before me, whose absences in colonial archives, as well as from

5   Poem by Dev Virahsawmy in Loga Virahsawmy, *The Lotus Flower: a conversation with Dev Virahsawmy* (Mauritius: Caractère Ltee, 2017), pp. 24–5.

family narratives, so strongly affected me? Many of Gouna's sisters, brothers and children are still alive and allowed me to capture stories, emotions and photographs as well as the 'non-stories' around the lack of interest in her as a woman in physical and mental pain. However, it was more of a challenge tracing the story of Gouna's mother, my great-grandmother, commonly known by her *non lakaz*[6] as Tantinn Tina or Kisnamah, something that still continues to intrigue me.

Tina

Not only did Tantinn Tina mother four boys and five girls – Ram, Gouna, Chris, Rajoo, Narain, Matee, Saroj, Jankee, and Devi – but she was married three times, which makes for as much of a fascinating story as the urge to know how she faced early twentieth-century society in the colony of Mauritius. Tantinn Tina was born more than a hundred years ago on 20 September 1904. On her birth certificate, recuperated from the Folk Museum of Indian Immigration, she is named Neelamah Dontula Runganaikaloo (Neelamah being her Indian paternal grandmother's surname, and Runganaikaloo her Indian father's surname). She was born on the Petite Rosalie Estate, a sugar plantation in the northern district of Pamplemousses, a few dozen kilometres to the north of the capital city of Port Louis. Retrieving her family's history was a real endeavour. Many archival facts were provided by a member of her side of the family, whom I traced through social media and by writing to many people with the name of Runganaikaloo born in Mauritius.[7] I chatted to a few young people whose families had been interested in the family lineage, usually patrilineal. By collating names, photographs and fragmented stories, I began to unearth and rearrange information into coherent narratives.

While I collected photographs of Gouna as a child in the 1930s and spoke to many aunts and uncles who grew up with her, I could only picture my great-grandmother, Neelamah (with the poetical meaning of Blue Mother) or Tantinn Tina, through the eyes of the younger generations for whom she was always a wife, a sister-in-law, a mother, an aunt, or a grandmother. Apart from her daughters and granddaughters, who spoke with great affection and pride of

6   This refers to the Mauritian tradition of using a person's nickname rather than their given birth name.

7   The Runganaikaloo family tree was meticulously retraced by Padma and Yves Moulin.

a resilient strong-minded woman, everyone seemed to regard her either with some form of veneration and respect, or with distance and coldness, even spite. She had three husbands after all, which was greatly frowned upon. I learned that she was made to work harder in the house as she was the first son's daughter-in-law. 'She always had a handkerchief and sweated a lot' was one intriguing detail I collected. She was incredibly beautiful, apparently, attributed to her fair skin and light eyes, 'despite her sisters and mother being very dark'. The prejudice of skin colour is inherent in this remark, reinforced by a structural racism inherited from colonial occupation. I also observed how women of the same generation rarely seemed to be supportive of each other. That matrifocal societies of care, sisterhood and female solidarities were broken in the colony also seems to be part of the mother wounds borne by each mother up to the time I came into being.

What I am doing here is what scholar Saidiya Hartman does in 'Venus in two acts':[8] arranging historical fragments and adopting the 'task of writing the impossible', a process which happens at the limits of the unspeakable and the unknown and is achieved through interpreting the silences and scraps of the colonial archive. The act of writing the personal demonstrates the limits of historiography or history writing through the act of narration or what she calls 'critical fabulation' (p. 11). To bring visibility and voice to the visceral story of Tantinn Tina, through others' interpretations, photographs, birth and death certificates, in parallel with the colonial historical and chronological narrative, was as challenging as it was rewarding.

One of the photographs that helped me capture an idea of the character of Tantinn Tina in the 1930s was a classic studio shot. Two wives sit in armchairs with a line of children on either side of them. Their husbands stand at the back in their ties and suits – copycats of colonial decency – like guardians and masters of their dynasty. Tantinn Tina, known for her much-admired light eyes, stares at the camera performing the role of the matriarch. Even through the sienna tones of the photograph, it can be discerned that she is quite fair. She is well-built and wears a light-coloured, long-sleeved, loose cotton blouse underneath what I think is a crispy raw cotton saree. I imagine the checks on her saree to be emerald green and rich brown with a wide blue-and-gold border. Her jewellery is ornate, yet subtly simple – a set of thick, heavy bangles, large ear studs and a necklace which, when I think about it, looks very similar to what Gouna is

8   Published in 2008 in *Small Axe: A Caribbean Journal of Criticism*, 12 (2): 1–14.

wearing in the picture of her at a similar time of life (stiff ring round the neck holding a rounded, shimmering triangular medallion in place in her suprasternal notch). I wonder if it is typical of the necklaces worn by married women from the South Indian region of Andhra Pradesh, Telangana, Odisha? In that picture, seven- or eight-year-old Gouna is sitting on a high studio prop, which is disguised as a bench, her hands cupped and placed quietly on her thin legs. Her mother Tina, however, sits comfortably in a rattan armchair, her left elbow resting gracefully on the arm-rest, her legs slightly apart under her saree. Her eyes are sharp and wide open and her lips slightly lazy, signs of resilience accompanied by a hint of defiance, as well as demonstrating her sense of entitlement as the wife of the eldest son. At least this is my reading of it.

I still wonder who Tantinn Tina's two ex-husbands were before she married for a third time and was brought to the entrepreneur culture of Quartier Militaire, where she gave birth to and mothered her nine children. I have discovered thus far that one of her husbands passed away. Migration under British colonisation represented a violent rupture from Indian tradition and rituals. In the process of being coerced into the indenture system Indian women were removed both from their castes and widowhood and thereby the meanings attached to these statuses. Instead they became expendable labour within the structures of plantation economies. Tina had apparently been in an abusive relationship, which she walked out of. She thus had no choice but to acclimatise to her third marriage and to integrate with the new class of workers who were interested in building livelihoods outside sugar-plantation labouring. Despite Tina's husband working as a sirdar in the fields, the family in Quartier Militaire owned a bakery, a bus transport business, a clothes shop, and rented a couple of houses in the locality (Tifrer being one of their tenants). The move from the sugar plantation was, for many, a way of resisting the colonial system of indentureship and focusing on accumulating wealth and building communities. When her husband died, Tantinn Tina, with the help of the meagre sirdar pension and some of her older children's earnings (all went on to work in different industries), diligently looked after her children until the youngest daughter was married. Tina eventually went on to live in Beau Bassin, one of the island's main towns, where lived her son, the kind-looking old man, he who thought I looked so much like his sister Gouna. Tina died of cancer in the mid 1960s, more than a decade after Gouna's death. I would have preferred not to focus solely on the marriages and motherhood of the women in my family, but it seems to have been an integral part of the colonial and patriarchal archive I was accessing. The traces left behind always seem to be connected to birth, marriage, motherhood and death.

Mariamah

Tina's mother, Mariamah – quite an uncommon first name, I might say, in the Mauritian context – was the first of my matrilineage to be born (23 December 1877) on Mauritian soil of Indian parents. Considering Mariamah's mother was called Utchamah (rituals related to Utchamah Kali are held in Mauritius), she could well have been named after Maariamma or Goddess Mariamman, who is considered to be the South Indian incarnation of Goddess Kali. The practice of reverence to the goddess indicates a society which built knowledges around a female-centred cosmogony, rituals which like (or unlike) the worship of pan-Indian Brahmanical goddesses, were brought to the colonies. These were demonised as folklore by a colonial (and patriarchal) epistemology. It is also probable that the Africanised Creole and the creative practices they brought to their language led it to flourish as a mother tongue in the rural areas where Indians recreated their lives. Those creative practices were culturally close to Mariamman worship songs which were also ad hoc hymns in the common language.

Mariamah Somanah was married to a South Indian man a decade older who came from Ganjam (Chicacole Gunjum India according to the colonial archive) with his parents when he was seven years old. I would like to believe that theirs was a nurturing relationship and that reconstructing diasporic lives in the colony was not an overwhelming task. I discovered she had five children from the age of twenty-two onwards, Tina being the third child, at their lodgings on the Grande Rosalie-Constance, a sugar plantation in the north of the island. The Rosalie estate of the eighteenth century (colonial houses always seem to have superfluous or feminine names) was the French Empire's colony centrepiece and comprised the dwellings of the governor and his entourage. In these days of the East India Company, they were passed down to descendants of French settlers under the British administration. I drove around the Grande Rosalie area in August 2017 and was struck by the fact that gated enclaves of bourgeois (white) privilege still occupy this wide stretch of land.

From the fragments of archival information available, I imagine Tina growing up in the humble lodgings provided for Indian workers in the yard situated at the back of the plantation space, and picture her children destined to work either in the colonial house or in the fields. The oppressive environment must have been completely different from the urbanised village-setting of Quartier Militaire. In 1908, when Tina was four and her youngest brother one, two Indian workers set fire to a range of huts on that estate in protest at the working conditions. The archives show that one of them appeared to claim that he was a silversmith and had not been recruited to work in the fields, and official documents state that the two workers wanted to have their contracts cancelled. The high rate of suicide recorded on the island allows the violence of and in the colony, and the harshness of the work imposed on Indians, to be visualised, such that to take your own life was considered preferable to enduring servitude akin to slavery and inhumane conditions. How much Mariamah knew the two protestors and was affected by the event can probably never be known. What I did find was that Mariamah's eldest son became a 'majordome' (butler) on the estate. I presume that, just as house slaves were regarded as having a higher status than field slaves in colonial hierarchical structures, being the master's butler must have been a better work fate than labouring in the sugar-cane fields. Whether Mariamah was proud of him I can only conjecture, but what I can deduce is that she seems to have supported her daughter during each of the two dysfunctional marriages Tina went through before her move to Quartier Militaire, as she welcomed her back home after each one failed.

From the birth and death certificates, it is clear that Mariamah, my great-great grandmother, must have come to the Petite Rosalie estate after getting married. The couple left the Mon Trésor and Union Vale plantations, situated in the south of the island at Grand Port, the places to which their Indian parents would have been 'dispatched' initially. Mon Trésor was a sugar plantation and factory close to the Union Vale estate. I remember this clearly from my colonial geography classes in primary school, where without a trace of the word 'colonisation', we had to learn about every sugar factory on the island. This could explain how both sets of parents got to know each other at some point, probably while working together in the sugar-cane fields and agreed, based on the proximity of their districts of origin in India (Odisha and Andhra Pradesh), that their children be promised in marriage to each other. More research might reveal that, having witnessed their parents having to work under such inhumane conditions at their respective estates, their children felt impelled to move to a different one on the other side of the island. The parents on both sides had come as couples (according to the colonial archive) in the space of a decade and neither returned to India after their indenture contracts. The big question is why? Did they want to go back? Were they pressured to stay? Did they think that going back to India would be shameful, as their lives in the colony of Mauritius were far worse than being at home and they had nothing to take back? Or did they decide to stay and consequently indigenise[9] the lands for the next generations?

Utchamah

My last step was to visualise Mariamah's Indian mother, Utchamah. Two documents summarise Utchamah's existence in the colony: information collected at her arrival in the Mauritian depot and her death certificate. The colonial registers record only one name for her: Utchamah. But a data entry, the number 297047, accompanies it. She seems to have been sent to the Union Vale estate with her 'husband' and probably spent some forty years in the new land of Mauritius. It has been well documented that most women who embarked on the indenture journey were widows and single women. Whether they were married, had previous children or decided at the depot or on the ship to be registered together, has yet to be uncovered. I can only speculate on the reasons why she embarked from colonial India on this journey to Mauritius, known as Maritch Desh. She left Rajamahendravaram, one of the largest cities in the East Godavari district and the birthplace of the eleventh-century poet Nannayya Bhattaraka, from whose work the grammar and script of the Telegou language and literature evolved. Despite feeling the need to poeticise this faraway place in the land of my ancestors, deep inside I am conscious of the daily struggle faced by those who were made to leave their towns, families, friends, communities and ways of life to embark on a passage to an unknown place: representatives of the wave of forced labour and involuntary migration intensively investigated by postcolonial literatures.

How much she missed her family and community (or not) back in India must again remain a mystery to me. And I can only

9　In her 1970 article, 'Jonkonnu in Jamaica: towards the interpretation of folk dance as a cultural process', philosopher Sylvia Wynter describes how enslaved people brought their knowledges and creative practices to the colonies and created new modes of survival and existence through, what she calls, a process of indigenisation. It was published in *Jamaica Journal*, 4 (2): 34–48.

speculate how much she reconstructed a similitude of that life on the island as a survival mechanism. Utchamah had Mariamah when she was forty years old which was, I think, quite late for motherhood in the context of her time and cultural background. It could also mean that Utchamah had other children before Mariamah. From what I can collate from her death certificate, Utchamah moved to stay with her daughter in her more advanced years and died there at the age of sixty-two in 1899. This was the year of her first grandson's birth and seven years before Tina was brought into existence by Mariamah, who had been born in the colony of Indian parents. I also wonder how she came to die at the northern estate to which her daughter had moved. Did mother and daughter leave together? Could she have moved to be with her daughter to continue the tradition of caring for her through pregnancy and beyond? Did she herself need to be taken care of? Did she suffer from mistreatment or abuse in her old age at the Union Vale and run away? Was she kicked out? Did she leave her husband (who was to die six years later)? Or did she unexpectedly die at her daughter's home, where her death is registered, on a visit to her daughter? These questions in themselves create histories.

Before writing this creative prose piece, I initially started to write the story of my family in the form of a poem following a chronological timeframe. I now end with that poem as a way of breaking linearity and of reclaiming a visceral history, one which does not belong to the past but to my present.

Name of immigrant: Utchamah
Immigrant no.: 297047
Name of father: Gooriah
Name of mother: ....
Name of ship: War Eagle
Distribution: 31. 01. 1863

Succinct. Perfunctory. Functional.

297047
[A data entry]. A classification//. A category:
Strategic mechanism of colonial order

Control, distribution
And redistribution

A number. With a notation.
A trace without a ~~body~~
Without a history
Without an individuation
From a colonial archive
Loaded with the silences
Of expendable labour
Muffled under the hypervisibility
Of glorified facts and dates

Name of this: ...
Name of that: ...
The organised naming - or rather unXnaming or re//naming
Of conquest and administration

While Utchamah's mother remains nameless
Dotted lines: ....
Empty, horizontal — — — —-, unimportant
Colonisation
Breaking matrifocal communities
Cutting links with ancestral wombs
Disembodying visceral knowledges
Erasing indigenous lands from history
Un-naming mothers and women   to   invisibilit

Utchamah was made of flesh and blood
Of history, culture and family
She left the town of Rajamahendravaram,
from the archive [Rajahmundry]
again renamed under British occupation of India.
And made a 600 kilometre
road journey to the port of Chennai.

We can only wonder why?
Famine/Poverty/Death?/Violence of colonial manipulation/under
the British 'experiment'/to extract labour/for sugar plantations/in
colonies across continents?

Or maybe the opportunity to migrate/find 'gold under stones'/
Under the promise of contracted work?

The drainage from this area
Seemed to have already started since 1837
      The year that Utchamah was born
      Three years after the start of the 'Great Experiment'/as it
was called
      Of trying to humanise enslaved labour from mainly Africa
      with indentured labour from India

      The colonial statistics quantifies
      200/- Indians from Rajahmundry
      Sent to labour in the sugar-cane fields
of the colony of Mauritius

The great experiment was never great
In 1839, it was suspended/Only to be renewed in 1842/under 'state'-
controlled policies devised/by British administrations in India and
Mauritius

when a 'Protector of Immigrants'
      was appointed to make
          a system of exploitation
              more   humane ....

Care&control
Always seem to go hand in hand

After long, precarious and uncertain weeks
crossing the Indian Ocean
Utchamah landed at Maritch
on the 28 January 1863.
She was 26.

For three days, she was quarantined
at the Immigration depot in Port Louis
Waiting to be distributed as colonial labour
in the form of 'wives to settle men'
or expendable worker in the plantation structure.

Her long family histories probably as
cotton weavers, land owners, jewellers, artists, carers
community teachers, leaders, doctors...
Erased under the new colonial order

She made it alive to a distant island
Which was always connected to the mother continents
As it forms part of Kumari Kandan
A mythicised lost underwater land
connecting Madagascar and India
Now proven true by the same system of knowledge
which made it a myth in the first place

Far away from exploitative humans
Although visited for centuries by Arabs and Africans
This island was however colonised from the seventeenth–twentieth
century/by Europeans/Who exterminated endemic animals/
Exploited resources/Then enslaved populations from Africa and
India/And contaminated the land with bitter sugar/A follow-up
from colonisation of the Americas since 1492

Utchamah was my Indian mother
My years in India as a student

And my trip to Hyderabad, Telangana
Did not bring me closer to her,
To her era or to her everyday life.

> Only the memories and the mother wounds
> Passed on for two centuries
> Across continents, oceans and generations
> Which I carry in my blood
> Brings us together
> At the present moment
> Forever intertwined in the past.

To the mothers I have retraced from the year 1837
Utchamah (1837), Mariamah (1877), Neelamah/Tina (1904) and Gouna (1925)

Mama Liberia

Angelica A. Oluoch

We have been home six full moons, now.

After three years in the white men's land, growing tobacco and sugar-cane and cotton.

Virginia, they called it.

Kamar will not remember much of it, for how young he is.

My thanks to Allah for that.

The ship brought us back, and left us with nothing.

No homes, no food, no kola nuts or palm wine to offer to our gods for the safe return of our children.

We returned with nothing.

Nothing but new names to gift our hands no longer bound by shackles:

Negro.

Nigra.

My Father the Teacher

Prithiraj R. Dullay

My father was born over a hundred years ago in 1906, in the Umzimkulu Sugar Mill compound that was situated on the north bank of the Umzimkulu River, which forms part of the Port Shepstone golf course today. As nineteen-year-olds, his parents had arrived from India as indentured labourers eight years earlier in 1898. Since my granny had little breast milk, a Zulu neighbour who had just had a baby, fed my dad on the one breast, while her own newborn suckled on the other! It is little wonder that the two youngsters became lifelong friends and referred to one another as 'milk brothers'. My dad would speak with great fondness and respect of his Zulu mother. In a few short years my father's three brothers and a sister followed.

When the 'three pound tax' on Indians was introduced by the government in 1913, Mohandas Gandhi called for a strike of all Indian sugar-plantation workers. Three pounds was six months' salary! My grandparents responded with enthusiasm. The Natal colonial government's response was equally swift. All the strikers were imprisoned for three months. That left my dad, only seven at the time, responsible for his siblings. Since money could buy little as there were no shops other than the company store, everybody relied on the food rations provided by the company and what little they could grow around the compound. With both parents in prison, there were no rations to be had. In reality my dad would not have managed at all, had it not been for his Zulu mother, who cared for her own three boys and took care of the five Dullay children for ninety days by eking out her own rations between them all. Other Zulu families in the compound also took in the children of the strikers, feeding and caring for them as well as their own. I was always amazed at my dad's fluency in Zulu. He sounded like a native speaker and was as deft at Zulu stick-fighting as his playmates. Neither his Zulu dancing nor his singing impressed me. Dad had the most unmusical voice and little rhythm in his movements but that did not deter him from participating with enthusiasm.

When the community started a school with one teacher imported from India, in the old Wilmot's building[1] in the village, dad was among the handful of children who attended. He had just three years of formal schooling, yet there was no suppressing his natural intellect and insatiable curiosity. His English was quite remarkable, since few spoke it in his environment. It later emerged that he had a love of languages. He conversed fluently in seven, including Hindi, Zulu, Urdu, Tamil, Telegu and even a smidgen of Afrikaans. Later in life many would bring him official documents or letters to read and explain. Sometimes neighbours asked him to write letters for them.

A year after dad was born the Port Shepstone harbour was abandoned when the single-lane road and rail-bridge extended the railway line into South Shepstone, just a kilometre from the river mouth. The new bridge severely restricted the navigability of the river and the harbour fell into gradual disuse.

As the children grew up, each was drawn from an early age into the plantation's labour force, first as helpers, later as workers in the mill itself or in the fields, or they became servants in the homes of the company managers. My grandfather and his equally tough and resourceful wife spent twenty-two years in the same plantation. They chose not to return to India. The salary for a grown man was ten shillings a month, paid in a single gold coin. The women were paid considerably less, although they worked equally hard. With the money they had saved and the severance pay, in lieu of the passage to India, they bought ten acres of land in the hilly Albersville area. They immediately cleared the lush tropical bush and farmed the two valleys where strong streams flowed. These became the rice paddy fields. Later the hilly slopes were also cultivated. My grandmother was the first to plant an orchard; it included twenty mango trees and a jackfruit tree as well as lychees, avocado, *naartjies* (mandarins) and pomegranate. The slopes were well suited to banana cultivation, paw paws and almost all kinds of vegetables. They had a few cows as well to supply their milk and butter needs. The first home was a collection of mud and wattle huts covered with thatch, the construction of which they had learned from their Zulu neighbours, while the main house of wood and iron was being built. Early on, the water supply was collected from the sparkling streams, and later it came from four massive water tanks which caught the rain water from the roof of the house. There was no electricity. Food was cooked on a large coal stove and paraffin lanterns provided lighting.

---

1   A business concern from the early 1900s which was no longer in operation.

My grandparents were incredibly resourceful and so were their children. Virtually nothing was impossible. My dad, who had worked in the crushing mill, was soon an expert in metal construction and problem solving. He had a white supervisor, who was almost always drunk. There was no supervision at all. He sat around dozing, while dad's ingenuity went to work. If a machine part was needed, he constructed it. If it required fixing, he sorted it out. His strength was Herculean. He learned welding skills and complex repair work. Soon he was regarded as being as good as the qualified white engineers, not that he was told so. When some machinery was needed urgently to keep production going, he often 'invented' what was necessary. In those far-off days it would take up to a year to get replacement parts. Transportation was primitive. It was still the era of sail and the early steam ships as well as the horse and cart.

My grandfather died after a short illness in 1924, when he was forty-five, just as the new wood and iron house was completed. The skills dad had learned were to prove invaluable later in life. By 1929, aged just twenty-three, he had bought a defective Harley Davidson, repaired it and toured Natal across tortuous, corrugated roads. I still have a picture of him astride the bike, cutting a dashing figure in his leather jacket.

As the family prospered, it was my granny who took control of the household and its finances. She was a formidable matriarch and brooked no nonsense from anyone. Her word was law. To oppose her in the slightest matter meant a tongue lashing that wilted her sons or their wives. Although she was firm, she also ruled her roost with fairness. She was always bare-footed. Thick brass anklets peeped from beneath her *langha* (skirt). She had similar brass bracelets on her wists, a nose-stud and the three-dot tattoo on her chin.

The farm yielded excellent vegetables and bananas which were sold at the village market. My dad's mechanical skills were in high demand. Since there was no public transport, one either walked or cycled, thus the time was ideal for the family to branch into the taxi business. It became so popular that soon there were two brand-new American Chevrolet taxis.

The family followed this in the mid 1930s by opening the first theatre, called the Shree Rama Hall, on the edge of the farm bordering the main corrugated Albersville Road of their small town. It staged all-night Hindu religious plays. A side income was earned from selling sweet tea and hot, salted nuts. It was not unusual for the plays to last ten hours or more. Eventually the theatre closed down and was converted into the town's first cinema, screening Indian and American films. Shortly after granny died in 1946, the hall was converted into a shop selling bicycles, accessories and spares as well as primus stoves. In the larger middle section was dad's workshop and right at the back was a radio and electrical repair shop, run by my oldest cousin, Ramdhini. In December of that year I was born.

By the standards of a small town, my family was quite well off. Our industriousness and the infectious attitude that radiated from dad about nothing being impossible laid the foundation for success. Like his mother, he brooked no nonsense but he had a warm and a caring heart. His business would have been a greater success had he not given 'credit' to the hundreds of poor neighbours and people from various 'native locations'. Much of this debt was never collected. Widows had little income and the unemployed had even less. Yet mouths had to be fed. That meant that dad provided food from our farm and helped with some cash. He gave away cabbages, aubergines, beans, mealies, yams and cauliflowers. To the Zulus he became *Baaba* (father) Ram and to others he became Uncle Ram. Automatically, I became *umfaana ka* Ram (the son of Ram) to everybody. His generosity became legendary. He used to say, 'When I die, can I take it all with me? Might as well use it to help people.'

Few people actually asked for help but dad was aware of the plight of each and every family. There was old Mrs Umaar from across the road and the widow Mrs Shorty Kathrada, with seven daughters and two sons. She sold *samoosas, murkoo* and *vaader* (Indian savoury snacks) to make ends meet. In order to save on purchased material, she sewed the top half of her daughters' traditional pants with soft cotton material salvaged from Blue Ribbon flour bags. When dad repaired her primus stoves and holey pots, she sent over a dozen samosas as payment. Often she could not even afford that. There were just too many mouths to feed. Dad didn't ask for money. Some of the African residents of one of the 'locations' mentioned above would come by to repair bicycles, purchased out of savings gleaned from their meagre earnings over many years. Payment would be six eggs or a live hen, depending on the complexity of the job. Often it was in the form of fruit or vegetables. Even the rich Mr Paulsen, the German dairy farmer from up the road, had his delivery bicycles repaired in return for tasty gouda cheese, milk and butter. This bartering of food for dad's services continued right into the 1960s. The businesses flourished in the 1950s and through the 1960s. In 1961 the family extended by renewing its interest in the cinema business and opening the Casa Cinema in Albersville, in partnership with the Naidoos and the Appalrajus.

I adored my dad. He was my great guru. He taught me his great love of the sea and of the plants and creatures around us. He taught me about the deadly green and black mambas, the scorpions and earthworms, as well as about the great aloes and wild fruit trees. He taught me about how the banana and date palms that dotted our coast grew luxuriantly in 'wild abandon'. I learned to cycle under his firm guiding hand and later to ride a motorbike. He taught me respect for all people and that racism was horribly wrong. He taught me honour, respect and fair play. From him I learned how to wield a stick to clear my path and to defend myself from snakes and from the huge, sneaky bush cats. My strong love of nature and great love for our coast was nurtured by him. He taught me about the myriad creatures of the tidal pools and about the great white sharks so abundant in our part of the world. Catching a large crayfish was an art that I learned early after several trials. Dad taught me about the tiny ghost crabs and sea lice as well as the massive blue-green crabs, caught mainly in the Izotsha Lagoon, using chicken intestines. He shared his love of the massive eels that tasted of chicken meat, which we caught in the muddy waters at the mouth of the Umzimkulu and how to skin them using ash.

Strangely, in school I was taught about the wonders of Britain, its empire and about snowy winters. Why was I taught about the winter snowstorms of Europe? I had not even seen a snowflake in my world. Nobody valorised our palms, aloes, the ferns and the lush subtropical vegetation. Later, I was to rationalise that everything European was at the top of the scale of values, and that all things from the colonised territories were at the bottom end of that scale.

When the Afrikaaner Nationalist Party came to power in 1948, they introduced draconian laws that brought most civil liberties to an end. What Nazism failed to implement in Europe, the Afrikaaners succeeded in doing in South Africa. One of its major targets was the banning of the Communist Party in 1950, making it illegal even to be a member. My radio-and-electrical-expert cousin, Ramdhini, used to set up a powerful short-wave receiver in our darkened lounge. At 8.30 on Sunday evenings the entire extended family gathered around the crackling receiver and tuned into the underground Communist Party's broadcast, possibly beamed from Moscow.

The Radio Freedom opening signature was the famous three dots followed by a dash. In my private act of subversion, I used to paint the Morse-like signature on to the wooden slats of tomato boxes and throw them on to the road. The broadcasts were barely audible due to the government's attempt to jam the signal. My child-mind shared in the family conspiracy by keeping totally silent throughout the clandestine programme. I had a delicious sense of fear mingled with the bravado of resistance. The same child-mind made us the 'good guys' versus the bad.

In the mid fifties dad adopted the Arya Samajist way of life. He gave up fishing and became a vegetarian. Swami Dayanand became his guiding spirit. The socialist ethos underpinning his teachings went down well with the way dad saw the world. This was to have a profound influence on my own life.

In 1962 the POQO[2] uprising began in Pondoland, in the Eastern Cape. The Xhosa people had had enough of the Apartheid Pass Laws, the laws that planned to restrict cattle ownership, and myriad other irksome laws. They revolted and lodged themselves in the mountainous areas, using whatever weapons were available – rifles and hand guns smuggled from Lesotho and even some dynamite stolen from the mines. The uprising lasted just a few months and was swiftly crushed by the apartheid state's military might. Without support from the rest of the country it was bound to fail.

It was during this time that some Xhosa 'farmers' one Sunday drove a battered *bakkie* (pick-up truck) carrying a huge load of firewood into the yard next to the repair shop. A few words were exchanged and dad opened the double front doors of the shop, let the bakkie in and quickly shut them again. I saw the two 'farmers' drag out a heavy package covered in hessian from under the bundles of firewood. They opened it and I could see guns. Dad told me to go down into the farm and play with my brother alongside the stream. I left reluctantly. Only later in life did I learn the full story. These were POQO guns that had jammed or were damaged in some way. Nobody in the Transkei could be entrusted with repairing them. Few black people in the country at that time had any engineering skills. More importantly, they needed to find someone they could trust. They had heard of Baaba Ram and of his being so skilled he could repair anything.

2   Meaning 'love' in Xhosa, this was the military wing of the Pan Africanist Congress (PAC).

At sunset when I returned from the farm with my brother, I could hear dad still hammering metal in the workshop. At 9 pm, I heard the bakkie splutter to a start and drive off. Dad washed, ate his late dinner and went to bed. I overheard him tell Mum in Hindi that he had fixed the guns for the Transkei comrades.

Some seven years later in 1969, when I was in my second year at college, dad was picked up by the security police and whisked off to the remote Voortrekkersstand in the Transkei for 'questioning'. We were frantic. He was gone for three days and nights then delivered to us in the early hours of the morning. He had been severely beaten and electrocuted. His face was swollen and one eye was almost shut. He told my mum to prepare home medication for his burnt fingertips. He gave away nothing to his captors. He knew nothing about gun repairs. Later he told me it was possible one of the 'farmers' had been captured and broke under torture. In the summer of that year, after he turned 63, he had the first of the cardiac problems that eventually took him off twenty years later, long after I had fled into exile. From my first year in college I started getting 'visits' from the Security Police. After all, I was the son of a terrorist suspect.

When I became an activist while at the Springfield College of Education in Durban between 1968 and 1970, I naturally leaned towards the philosophy of black consciousness, espoused by Steve Biko. I refused to have my humanity negated by a people who, while acknowledging their own, denied it to people of colour. The arrogance enraged me and fed a well of resistance deep within.

In 1969 when I returned home for the summer holiday, I talked at length to dad about 'politics' while we sat under the shade of the Jaamun-madoni trees at the side of our home. I explained the philosophy of black consciousness and why it had great appeal for me. I talked about the massacre at Sharpeville and Langa and the bannings of the ANC (African National Congress) and the PAC (Pan Africanist Congress) as well as the ominous silence in mounting resistance to the restrictions. As afternoon drew into evening, I spoke of our sense of near betrayal; of the anger many felt against their parents, and of Apartheid's dehumanising processes. He saw my anger and his response was understanding and not admonishing. He talked of the power of the white government and its allies in the west. His closing words that afternoon were that, although we had found a new way of looking at the struggle, we should still remember the Maureens[3] of our country and the fact that not all white people were demons. I was not too pleased with that, given my conversion to the new consciousness. Where were Maureen and her ilk when we were being tortured and beaten senseless? The National Union of South African Students did not live my reality as a black person. They could only theorise and perhaps sympathise then return to their white world of privilege. No white political party spoke of the sheer horror of what Apartheid did to the lives of ordinary people. In the late 1960s the South African economy boomed and no liberation struggle was going to dent that. White South Africans had the highest living standard in the world. Californians came a poor second. That, according to the Afrikaaner Nationalist Party government, was worth defending.

In the meantime we were engrossed in defining our identity and increasing awareness of the irrelevance of Apartheid state power. Whites were to become inconsequential to our struggle. It was time for the piper to play a different tune.

A militancy was born that was to carve out a new destiny for South Africa.

---

3   Maureen, a white childhood acquaintance also from Port Shepstone, is featured in another of my stories.

Gandhi and the Girmitya

Satendra Nandan

Mohandas Gandhi in the twentieth chapter, Part 2, of his An Autobiography: the Story of my Experiments in Truth *writes about his sudden encounter in South Africa with a stranger, a 'coolie' named Balasundaram. That unexpected meeting was life-changing for Gandhi and led to the abolition of the indenture system, almost a century ago.*

He'd proclaimed:
God is Truth.
'No?'
He whispered;
And changed his mind–
It's the other way round:
Truth is God.

When one is young one makes mistakes.
The dandy lawyer
In three-pieces of silk,
Always after nothing but the whole truth!
Then he began spinning
The wheel of fate
Or fire?
It's difficult to tell
From this distance.

But truth is never far away.

One fine morning
As he sat in his attorney's office
– London-trained and attired –
Shuffling legal papers

For litigious merchants,
Entered Balasundaram—
In ragged coolie clothes –
Bashed, battered, bleeding
Two front teeth broken
A godforsaken creature
Blood driveling from his lips.

Below the crinkled skin, a human face,
Carrying his safa, turban,
In both his hands
And babbling Tamil, his mother's tongue.
It wasn't an offering
Or a greeting but a plea:
Do something for us too:
We cannot pay our dues
To be members of a rich congress.

Gandhi was moved
By the labourer's dignity, and the soiled clothes.
How shall I spin this one?
The General in his labyrinth is strong:
What decency has ever won against general smut?

The white doctor, the white magistrate
Their righteous indignation aroused
Against the white employer.
If I tell the truth,
Others will be truthful too.
That is the only basis of our lives.
Balasundaram was given to another employer:
He was a bonded coolie again.

It's an ordinary story, a relic,
In any lawyer's office
Among tattered and frayed files,
A daily occurrence,
From South Africa to the South Pacific,
And the crossings of the Atlantic.

But a strange thing happened:

As Balasundaram
Took off his blood-stained scarf from his head
Gandhi saw more than most;
His heart's desire was fulfilled
To serve strangers in strange places.
He changed his sartorial tastes
Shaved his hair himself:
The coolie barrister
Became a coolie!
And began to spin
A thread that reached the Cross
On a hill between two thieves
And to a god exiled on Everest.

Miracles happen when the soul
Of a coolie
And a mahatma become one.

Balasundaram had given him a truth:
How can men feel honoured
In the humiliation of their fellow beings?

It was not a question he asked.
It was the answer he found
From the bleeding mouth of a coolie.
From then he began to spin
Closeted in the dust of his skin
The threads of many freedoms
When a coolie had morphed into a mahatma.

Then they shot him dead –
Three steel bullets of rusted iron.
'He Ram!'
Was all he mumbled –
Two words, the last three letters of a coolie name.

And Balasundaram stood:
Alone by Sabarmati's shore
He knew the river had changed its course
But not ceased its flow
And history had happened.
Miracles, too, are sudden, inexplicable,
Like births or assassinations.

His head held high
His white turban shining like a star,
Next to a slice of the moon,
In his folded palms:
His heart without fear
On his face a single tear
His bare head in its last homage:
That this beauty is beyond human breath:
Even he saw it too late
In silence: that one death sometimes
Makes us all ONE
Nobler than we are.
And gives us Life in our lives.

Pepsi, Pie and Swimming Pools in-the-Sky

Cynthia Kistasamy

My father was a carpenter. When I was young, my mother would tell me that Jesus had been a carpenter too. Before he had received the word of God and become a Messiah, he had been a carpenter first.

My father was a salt-of-the-earth, blue-collar worker. Each day he would come home smelling of clean sweat and sawdust. It was a smell that clung to him even after he grew old and retired. It was a scent best described as fresh pine cones and damp earth. As a child, one of my chores each day was to unlace his boots and fetch his sandals when he came home from work and plonked himself down on his red comfy-chair in our living room.

His long socks, as I rolled them down the wide girth of his legs, would make small clouds of dust around his feet. These clouds smelt sharply of the freshly sawed wood and lacquer he had been working with that day.

One day my father rustled in with a large, white shopping bag. I heard him tell my mother that Mr Wright, his boss, had not had time to go out Christmas shopping for his kids that day, so he had sent my father out with a list instead. Errands like these were a common part of my father's job.

Intrigued by the plastic bag in the corner of the room, I kept peeking inside. Mother shooed me away each time, but it was my father who eventually said that I could open the bag.

'You may take the things out and have a look', he conceded, 'but don't open the packaging.'

Gingerly, I opened the bag. Inside lay a bundle of marvels. There was a G.I. Joe action figure, a ThunderCats costume mask and a plush Cabbage Patch Doll. But of all the treasures inside, it was the Smurfs play-set that enthralled me the most. The play-set was a complete replica of the entire Smurf village, including all the little blue characters, each piece placed inside a box which was wrapped in fragile cellophane plastic.

There were even tiny red toadstool houses of varying sizes, with small white dots on them.

I had never seen anything so enchanting before.

All that evening I played delicately with the box wrapped up in clear plastic. I was like Lemuel Gulliver discovering a new Lilliputian world. I kept gliding my clumsy fingers over the delicate plastic, swept into that place where only children dwell.

Smurfette, with her fine gold hair and high-heeled shoes was my favourite. At bedtime I put the toys safely back into their white packet.

In the morning, the packet was gone and I did not think of it again until much later.

As a child, I knew not to ask for such gifts. I had no illusions of receiving such extravagances. Children like me didn't play with such beautiful things.

My gifts were always of the practical sort. A new set of clothes at Christmas time, a box of colour pencils for my school box, a packet of Love-in-Tokyo hair ties to keep my hair tidy.

Sometimes, I would think about the children who did receive toys like those in the plastic bag and I would envy them.

In time, I learned that errands run for Mr Wright didn't always keep office hours. Nor did they apply just to my father. They were also not considered errands by Mr Wright. He called them 'favours'.

Once a month, Mr Wright would ask that my mother do him the 'favour' of cooking a pot of curry for guests he was entertaining at his home over the weekend. Mr Wright would say that my mother made the best curry ever. In his presence, my mother would smile coyly at his remark. But at night, when alone with my father, I would hear her bark at him about the audacity of 'that man'.

She would say, 'They like our curry, they like our culture, yet they still treat us like second-class citizens. Why do you put up with this nonsense, John?'

John was the English name given to my father as a boy. His birth name was Krishna but it proved to be too much of a tongue-twister on the lips of the Wrights, who had served as employers to my father's family for generations. They cleverly skirted the problem of troublesome native names by changing them to something that rolled off the English palate more fluidly.

It had always been a bizarre thing to behold; these dark-skinned, Tamil-Tiger men in my family, dressed in over-the-knee safari socks and *kort-broekje*,[1] sipping on Black Label beer and conversing with their heavily accented, Mother-India tongues. And then to hear them refer to each other by biblical names such as 'Jacob', 'Moses' or 'John'. Even as a child I felt there was something quite unnatural about it.

In these scuffles with my mother, my father would always remain calm and I would hear the same flat response to her question every time.

'Rooks', he'd say, 'you don't have to do it if you don't want to. Just let it be okay?'

At the end of these little spats over 'that man', my parents always decided that my father's job was too important to lose over a pot of curry. In the end, at least once a month, my mother would spend the morning in the kitchen cooking curry, which my father would deliver, with a smile, at the doorstep of Mr Wright's home.

Another monthly ritual, but one we all enjoyed, was the shopping trip to Hypermarket-by-the-Sea. It was one of the biggest supermarket stores in Durban in the eighties. My mother would dress me up in frilled bobby socks and we would all climb into my father's little blue Peugeot and drive from our house in the village to Hypermarket-by-the-Sea.

The forty-minute trip to Hypermarket-by-the-Sea was a treat on its own as it followed the coast. We would leave behind the streets with their tiny, uniform council houses, and the landscape would change as we moved closer to the city. Brown drabness turned to lush, green terrain with the warm Indian Ocean as its backdrop. Houses became bigger and more opulent as we drove along the coast, heading towards the city.

My dad's blue Peugeot would motor along past picture-perfect houses with palisade fences and iron gates. For a time, it was a game of mine to count the swimming pools as we passed by each house. I would be on the alert for little flashes of blue rectangles, briefly and barely visible through the bars of gates, or through gaps in the house fences.

Blue rectangles would whirl by. My count would begin – one, two, three…

1   Afrikaans word meaning 'short pants'.

It was through these car trips to the city that I learned to equate wealth with owning a swimming pool. Nobody where I came from had swimming pools in their yards, or even knew how to swim for that matter. The mere thought of it was absurd!

I would wonder about the people who lived there in swimming-pool-land. I would picture them in summery bathers and floppy hats, laughing nonchalantly and frolicking with big, fluffy dogs in their pristine gardens. These must be the houses of the ever-deserving children who received extravagant gifts.

After our shopping, my dad would treat us to pie and gravy at the little canteen just inside the massive store's entrance. I would always get steak pie and a bottle of cold Pepsi. We ate our pie in plastic plates, with plastic knives and forks, seated at plastic tables with plastic chairs.

In our house, we always ate food with our hands. As Indians, this is how we eat. Yet when I sat down for our once-a-month pie and Pepsi, my father always insisted that I eat with the plastic knives and forks provided in square basins, along with paper napkins and sachets of tomato sauce, placed near the till counter.

For a time, I harboured the thought that my father had been embarrassed about our customary way of eating our food. Perhaps he felt that, to the other patrons sitting around us, we'd look too Indian, too foolish and ill-refined.

One day, when we were both much older – he a retired widower and I a high-school graduate – we were conversing casually, reminiscing about the past. I asked him why he had insisted on me using those horrendous, flimsy implements when we ate pie at Hypermarket-by-the-Sea. As a child unaccustomed to utensils, it took me forever to cut those pies into little pieces and spear them into my hungry mouth. But my father had been adamant. No knife and fork, no pie.

'Where you that ashamed of our "Indian-ness", dad?', I had teased.

He seemed surprised by my question, but then chuckled.

'Of course I wasn't ashamed', he smiled. 'I was preparing you for a life that I wished for you, a life better than mine. I knew that one day you could use these skills in places I'd never go to, places I'd never see in this lifetime. This has always been my wish for you. My wish is that of a life of inclusion, a world that is friendly and yours to enjoy at your leisure. A world that you would someday own.'

People usually have at least one light-bulb moment in their lifetime. This was mine; the realisation that the world was my oyster, its soft fleshy folds there for me to coax open and explore. Its embedded pearl waiting to be found.

His words rang most clear the day I watched, on our TV set, Tata Madiba and Winnie walk hand-in-hand out of the Victor Verster prison gates, the world dancing to the beat of freedom.

Today, I am a big-time project manager relocating to the city of Johannesburg to take up a post at a well-known engineering firm. As I look for a new house here in the city, I find that my first question to any estate agent is, 'Does the house have a swimming pool? It must have a swimming pool and it must be in the shape of a rectangle.'

The fact that I cannot swim is irrelevant. There must be a pool.

Escape from El Dorado: a bittersweet journey through my Guyanese history

Anita Sethi

Sweetness seeps through my ancestral story, quite literally, for if it was not for humans' hunger for sugar centuries ago, I would not ultimately have been born. This is a story more bittersweet than saccharine though, interweaving the personal and historical. I have long had a sweet tooth and as I grappled with my fraught relationship with sugar I unfolded journeys within journeys: I went on a long voyage – by turns intensely pleasurable and piercingly painful – from a hospital bed where I was forced to examine the roots of my history with sugar, to childhood memories of devouring sweets in my grandmother's corner-shop in Manchester, to the vast sugar-cane fields of Guyana where my ancestors once toiled as Indian indentured labourers. I discovered that the history of sugar was intrinsic to the story of my family, many miles from Manchester. I learned how thousands of Indians including my ancestors ended up in Guyana during the 1800s, having been shipped there to work as indentured labourers, and that is where my mother was born in 1948. I discovered how, following the abolition of slavery, people across the world were brought, in a mass movement, to work on plantations, often under false pretences – sold a dream of a good home and job but finding only a nightmare.

I walk by the waterways in my hometown of Manchester, United Kingdom, looking at the moonlight reflected in the Manchester Ship Canal. As I walk, I wonder about the many journeys that have been made upon this canal which once carried cotton. So many millions of tonnes were shipped from across the world that the city came to be known as Cottonopolis. I follow the gleaming water as it flows into the Bridgewater Canal and into the River Irwell, yearning to follow it right to the sea to uncover its many mysteries. As I walk, I wonder too about other world waterways flowing through my ancestry and the vast journeys human beings have made upon them, journeys forced and journeys chosen, journeys of slavery, indenture and freedom. As I walk, memories stir and swell. The past ebbs and flows.

The word 'Guyana' derives from an indigenous Amerindian language meaning 'land of many waters', and there certainly is an abundance of waterfalls flowing through the country. Along with the natural waterways there is also a canal system, a legacy of colony. It was there in that land of many waters that my mother was born, in what was then British Guiana, in a village in Berbice near a muddy-brown river upon which huge waterlilies floated. Following Independence she journeyed alone to England, aged twenty-one, to undertake a nurse traineeship, arriving one bitterly cold winter.

It was in Manchester a few years later that her waters broke and I was born, a direct product of British colonial history. Yet I met many who had never heard of Guyana. Growing up the daughter of a Guyanese mother, confusion would meet me when I answered the question, 'Where are you from?' 'Where, Ghana?', people would reply – it seemed as if my mother country was not even on the map, at least not in the map people hold in their minds. It had, seemingly, been washed from history. The subtleties of Guyanese culture were also lost on people. Although my mother was brown, she did not fit neatly under the umbrella of 'Asian'; she had a Guyanese accent and cooked Indian food – but with a distinctly Guyanese flavour. Continually explaining my identity, which seemed to live beyond the edges of clearly defined categories, could be exhausting.

The fiftieth anniversary of Guyana's independence from British colonial rule was marked in 2016, and the hundredth anniversary of the abolition of indentured labour in 2017, yet how much do we really know and understand about Britain's colonial history? I remember being taught nothing as a child in history lessons about this part of Britain's past. I was taught nothing of how in the nineteenth century following slavery indentured labourers known as 'Gladstone coolies' – including my own ancestors – were shipped to British Guiana from British India to toil on plantations, nor anything about the legacy left by indenture and colonialism. I can only guess at whereabouts in India my mother's ancestors originated: during my visit to the archives, I could not discover the relevant records. So much has vanished from history and there are no meticulously preserved documents for this period. Furthering this sense of erasure and amnesia, the country was seemingly forgotten after Independence, remembered mainly for the Jonestown massacre.[1] It briefly made the newspapers when Prince Harry included it on his 2016 Caribbean tour itinerary.

---

1   The mass murder-suicide in 1978 of 918 religious cult members (including many children) of the Peoples Temple, led by the reverend Jim Jones.

'You put me in a box and you don't know who I am. How dare you presume to know who I am?', declared the Guyanese campaigner Gina Miller, responding to UKIP's Patrick O'Flynn. Born in what was then British Guiana, she has faced a torrent of racist abuse, death threats and demands that she leave the country. It is imperative that we understand our country's colonial history, which brought people of colour to Britain, to eradicate the deep-seated ignorance that breeds prejudice and racism.

I yearned to uncover the secrets hidden in my history, to fill in the gaps in my narrative. In childhood a map of the world was tacked to the wall, with the place where my mother was born encircled. I wanted to make my history more than two-dimensional, to see and taste and smell the place for myself. Before travelling to my mother's birth country, I consulted contemporary and historical maps of the region to gain a sense of its contours and evolution. But we also carry with us the inner mappings of memory and myth. Would my emotional and imaginative maps alter as I journeyed? And would I discover more about my ancestors' treacherous journey as indentured labourers, and what life was like for them toiling in plantations?

As I walk near the Manchester Ship Canal, other waters rise in my memory. I remember staring over the precipice into one of the highest waterfalls in the world, the Kaiteur Falls, crashing into mist. I felt vertiginous not only because of the vast height and stomach-churning depth beneath, but also due to the huge swell of history around me, much of it shrouded in mist. I reflect on the mist-and-myth-wreathed Mount Roraima, the highest mountain in Guyana, which inspired Sir Arthur Conan Doyle to write *The Lost World*. For as well as once being home to my mother, the Guianas were once thought to be home to the lost city of El Dorado and lured the British, French and Dutch in search of gold. In the sixteenth century, Sir Walter Raleigh set sail in search of El Dorado, the fabled city of gold – he never found it. I wanted to make my own journey to my maternal country and move beyond the mist and myths shrouding it.

*

'Sugar was like gold', my mother remembers, about growing up in Guyana. Little wonder that the El Dorado myth persisted through the centuries for there was gold of a different sort to be found – those sweet, sparkling crystals. My mother remembers how the sugar-cane surrounding her childhood home was so 'razor-sharp' that it would cut the fingers if not touched carefully. I've also learned other ways in which sugar can hurt.

Then there is the enormous journey of those tiny sparkling crystals: from the cane fields of Demerara, to the packet of Demerara sugar out of which the sweetness is neatly poured and stirred into the teacup of someone thousands of miles away, often oblivious to that extraordinary journey. The story of sugar is interwoven with that of my own life. This story does not often leave a sweet taste in the mouth, as it traces the journey of the exploited people who travelled across the earth as indentured labourers to work in the sugar-cane fields. Such was the fate of my ancestors on my mother's side of the family who made the treacherous journey across the world hoping for a better, sweeter life, but meeting grinding hardship in those fields.

'A despotism tempered by sugar' was the term used by the novelist Anthony Trollope to describe British Guiana's sugar plantocracy, an observation modified by one magistrate in 1903: 'It seemed to me more like a despotism *of* sugar'. One example is the Booker family, who owned sugar plantations in Guyana from the early nineteenth century – the same Booker family who lend their name to the Man Booker Prize for Fiction. People living and working on the plantations, and the generations that came after them, felt the pain not just the pleasure of sugar.

It was about an hour's drive through Berbice to the sugar-cane estate in Canje. My cousin and I cruised past place names such as 'Adventure', and the sight of a town called 'Manchester' made my heart skip a beat at the memory of home thousands of miles away, for it was in my hometown of Manchester that my sweet tooth developed. My grandmother owned a corner shop filled with sweets and chocolate which curved around a corner of Stretford, on the same road as the Lancashire Cricket Ground. We called it 'Mama Shop', my grandmother being known to us as 'Mama'. Every day she would work in the shop, which sold an assortment of confectionery and groceries – it was the former that interested me most. I remember the sensation of those sugar-filled sweets, the chocolate melting in the mouth, teasing the tongue. I remember the jars filled with glittering, sugar-encrusted sweets in a myriad of bright colours, a feast for the eyes on the greyest of days. I remember how they had other uses aside from being eaten: the love-heart necklaces to drape around the neck, the ring-shaped sweets to slide upon a finger, the bracelets made of sweets to hug the wrist – I spent my childhood not only eating sugar but wearing it. Then there were the sweets forbidden to me at a young age: bubble-gum, for example, which I would slip into my mouth clandestinely, trying to chew discreetly as the sweetness gradually drained away. I would dream of the liquorice laces, lollipops, refreshers, the snap-and-crackles fizzing and exploding on the tongue.

It was centuries after my ancestors' extraordinary journey that my own sweet tooth finally got the better of me, and prompted me to take a good long hard look at the inflamed roots of my relationship with the sweet stuff and investigate its history. I was in hospital, attached to a drip, with intravenous antibiotics and painkillers flowing through my veins, and was forced to think deeply about my complex history with sugar – not only the history of my three decades of life, but also of the decades stretching back before my lifetime. What had once been hugely pleasurable had turned into pain. I lay in a hospital incapacitated by my sweet tooth. The reason seemed somewhat embarrassing: the urgent need for root canal treatment. I was decaying, or at least a tooth of mine was, and that decay had spread to the very roots, so it could only be fixed by killing the nerves of that sweet tooth. Such a small part of the body could cause such great pain. It was sugar that had caused all this hurt. Sugar was to blame. It was only after emerging from the most intense hotspots of pain that I could think again, that I could remember, that I could explore the roots of my craving for sweetness.

What are the roots that clutch?

So asked a wise poet many years ago. As I recall how my roots were cleansed and the rot removed, I consider how important it is to examine the very roots of who we are. My recollections of root-canal treatment bring to mind the canal system of Guyana, a legacy of colonialism. Waterways were dug by the enslaved and, after the 1838 abolition of slavery, Indian indentured labourers continued excavating the earth, digging and draining. Canals ran through the coastal plantations, to the river, to the sea.

I wanted to search for my roots, to excavate deep into the painful past. So here I was, thousands of miles from Manchester in the UK, on a journey to a sugar estate in my mother's hometown of Berbice, passing through a place called Manchester in Guyana, prompting these memories. As the sun blazed down and we got stuck in

Saturday market-day traffic, I looked out at huge watermelons and mangos lining the roadside and saw a van with the words 'LIFE GOES ON' on its windscreen. Life rolled on as we drove along the straightest road in the whole of the Caribbean, without a single kink or curve. We drove on past rice fields, chocolate-brown rivers with huge lilies floating upon their surfaces, passing wooden houses raised from the earth by stilts, to reach the sugar-cane estate, Rose Hall, the headquarters of the Guyana Sugar Corporation. I looked at smoke curling out of the factory and, beyond it, more fields of sugar-cane as far as the eye could see. What I remember most is the bitter-sweetness of the smell: the air thick with the cloying smell of sugar mixed with the acrid, oily smell of the industry itself. It was hard to breathe in for long. I thought of those who breathed this polluted air before me, of every breath my brave ancestors took.

It was almost enough to put me off having sugar in my tea ever again, not only the overwhelming sickly-sweet smell, but imagining the harsh realities of indentured labourers' lives in the nineteenth century. Conditions have somewhat improved, with more workers' unions, compared to the days when indentured labourers toiled beneath the burning sun, herded into ranches like cattle, all to sweeten the blood and line the pockets of their masters. Visiting the cane fields where workmen produce Demerara sugar, and understanding the processes which take this substance from field into food made for a bittersweet day. It was a stark reminder of where the food we eat comes from, and the long journey it makes.

As we were walking through Skeldon, my cousin told me how sugar is made from raw sugar-cane and outlined the many stages in the extraction process. I saw the country with new eyes: how sugar infiltrated the everyday, from the street sellers peddling toddy made from water and sugar-cane juice, to the diabetes crisis cutting lives short (since it is cheaper to drink Coca-Cola than access clean drinking water). Heated debates are now taking place throughout the western world on the need for a 'sugar tax'.

I called this piece 'Escape from El Dorado' as it is both an attempt to untangle the myths that the past attracts – often detracting from real truths – and an attempt to free myself of the shackles of the past through understanding it. Knowledge is indeed power, but knowledge was snatched from us by the loss of many historical documents about indentured labour, and there is a woeful lack of awareness in the UK concerning the truth about indenture, colonialism and empire. There is so much more to learn about my ancestors' journey from India to toil as indentured labourers in the sugar-cane plantations of Guiana; so much erased from history that must be painstakingly rediscovered. The hidden horrors and heartaches of history must be remembered. As I walk by the Manchester Ship Canal, as I wander and wonder, I feel that ebb and flow of time, without me and within me.

Talanoa[1] with my Grandmother

Noelle Nive Moa

She roused me from my sleep, my grandmother small and sweet
To tell me a tale of love torn apart, by a time so long past.
She touched her lips to my head, my grandmother small and sweet,
And so began her story, of a time so long past.

His hair was a trail of silken black,
A moonless path that wound its way around his back.
He'd heard the siren's call, he sailed forth
The heady sound of the drums
Of the navigators beating against the shore.

Two years he'd toiled these lands for men,
Foreigners in this foreign land they were,
Though it was his hands that tore and bled,
His back that bent.

They crossed the *Tepre Pacificum,*
Frigate birds soared, their wings carrying salt and wind.
They sailed into Apia Harbour in the Year of the Monkey
SS *Progress* had borne them away from home.
The posters had promised fat bellies and fat riches.
Sign away three years to fulfil those promises,
Promises in a land of promise.

Two years he'd toiled these lands for men,
For foreigners in this foreign land they were,
Men of snow and steel, tempered in the fire of these volcanic
islands.

1   (Tah-lah-noah). Samoan term for talking or speaking; a conversation

His hands tore apart the fibrous husks of coconuts
Extracting oil for palagi² candles, palagi lamp fuel, palagi soaps.
Two years he'd toiled these plantations
Three years he'd signed away
Promises in a land of promise.

She saw him on a Sunday, on Taufusi Road.
One day to congregate, gamble and gossip,
These bound men so like a group of old ladies, lo'omatua.³
They were forbidden to speak to them these labourers,
Forbidden by their own prejudices, by their own fear.
But rules are to be broken.
She met with him in secrecy
Ignoring the taboos of her people
Ignoring those that ruled over her people.

And so in love they were they married
And so she was disowned by her family
And so she had brought shame on her people
And so she was banished.

Three more years he signed away
And thrice more he would sign again.

Archdukefranzferdinandcarlludwigjosephmaria
What is this name to the people of the ocean?
These strange foreign palagi names
That have no bearing on our forebears
And yet their hands stay our fate
Chastising us like children
Bent to the caprices of the absent parent.

---

2 (Bah-lung-gnee). Samoan term for a European person.
3 (Loa-o-mah-too-ah). Samoan term for an old woman/old women.

Three more years he signed away
But this new guard said nay
They tipped their rifles towards the east
And ordered them away
They begged, they cried
They held their matrimony aloft
But the new guard turned their heads
Indifferent and unmoved
Their fate was set adrift.

She climbed the highest peak
And watched him sail away
She had no more tears left
And for weeks she would not speak
Of his name, of her pain
For this was hers alone.

She roused me from my sleep, my grandmother small and sweet
She brushed a trail of silken black gently across my cheek
She roused me from my sleep, my grandmother small and sweet
So that I may hear a tale of a time so long past.

Passage from India

Anirood Singh

Sundown; me 'n Arthi at the Ocean Terminal, sweating on the T Jetty in Durban's midsummer, air as warm as my alcohol-tainted blood. The Indian Ocean laps against the concrete piers coated black 'n white with foul-smelling barnacles. The Duke's Combo plays *Theme from a Summer Place*; sweet like a lemon. Dee Sharma's saxophone lulls me into dreaming. My eyes scan over the mysterious water, foolishly peering to see the hulk of the Indian subcontinent from which emerged the first cargo-load of indentured labourers, landing on the Dark Continent in 1860, a hundred-and-one years ago.

Here we are, fourth and fifth generation, walking hand in hand. My only child frowns up at me.

'*Pāpāji*, why are you smiling?'

'Oh, *betī*, just thinking 'bout my great-grandfather's journey over the Hind Mahasagar[1] in search of survival or adventure, without a plan or map...'

'Tell me his story.'

'It's a long, boring one that will not interest an eight-year old.'

'I like to learn our family history, especially where we came from.'

'Okay, *merā pyarā larkī*.[2] Now, if you want a dramatic *kisa*, I'll have to be an actor and play the role of my *pardādā*, Ashok Viśvās. I'm going to make it up from what he and my *ājā* told me, and what *bāba* translated from Hindi into English in this big black notebook he called his *Ramayana*.'

'Pāpā, you went to school, learnt English ... how long?'

'Yes, ma'am; twelve years. I got a Matric Certificate.'

'Then why talk English mixed with Hindi?'

---

1   Indian Ocean.
2   'My beautiful girl.'

'It's called spicing up the bland *Aṅgrēzī* dish', I laugh. 'But really, I want you to learn the language of your ancestors, if only a little.'

Arthi nods, and then frowns. 'What is your story's title?'

I kiss her on the forehead. '*Passage from India*, by Rohit Viśvās. Now, *betī*, rem'ber, out of respect, we don't use the names of our elders, but I'll have to do it for the story's sake.'

My sole audience nods.

We settle down on a concrete bench marked 'Europeans only – Slegs Blankes'[3] near the edge of the jetty, water on three sides. I hold my only possession of value, born a minute before my *patnī* died. I wipe a tear, sniff.

'First, an introduction: I was eleven when Ashok died, aged 73. I rem'ber his white turban with matching beard and thick walrus moustache, telling tales with a crooked smile and the occasional draw on the hookah.' I clear my throat; open the home-made storybook.

*

The main thing I rem'ber is the thirst, I can swallow nothing. My throat burns, stomach makes noises, nose itches from the bad, bad smell like one madman mixed salt, sweat and piss. We hardly see anything, but hear dirty, half-naked men grumbling, sighing, farting and puking, competing with the ship's non-stop creaking. The *jahāz* may be complaining of the weight of so many Indian men, a few women and children, it has to carry for some five-six weeks. I feel in my guts the never-ending rolling, making me look like someone who drank too much home-made *dharoo*, or pulled long and hard on the *chīllum*. I've been lying down, day 'n night, night 'n day, for weeks, so weak, sick, want to throw up, but my stomach's got nothing to vomit.

To take my mind off my grumbling stomach, I think of the place where they said diamonds sparkle in the sand, gold shines on the sides of roads and grows on *baiṅgan* plants. Ah, the Promised Land for Indian coolies, the British colony of Natal, at the bottom tip of Africa. It might as well be on the dark side of the moon.

*

3   'Whites only'.

'*Pāpāji?*'

'Yes, *betī?*'

'Is this a fairy tale?'

I laugh. 'The story may sound like one, but it's true. That's how we came to be here.'

'Okay.'

*

My clever brother, Jhora, five years older'n me, said he'd rather be a fool and believe the fantastic stories of *hirē* and *sona* than see, feel, hear, taste, and smell life wasting away in our miserable *gaon*. *Bāba* said we must stop thinking 'bout nonsense and work harder on his small sugar-cane plantation, knowing full well that we'll never get enough pay from Bapū Dulelsing to whom *pitāji* always sold his crop.

One day, me, father, and Jhora visit Bapū. We suck sweet, hot tea from the saucer as we listen to him saying there's no future in Goshukigurh, not even in the District of Agra. His son, Bodasing, is going with his blessing to find a job on a sugar plantation in Natal. Even if that place is a jungle with lions, elephants and all, it'll be better than staying and starving in Bharat. Father tells us if we want to go, he won't stop us.

Jewellery shop-owner, Cohen sahib, who made money within pān-spitting distance of the Taj Mahal, said, 'Live in this Godforsaken barren village, you'll die slowly from chronic malnutrition and dust in your lungs. Or go, boys, to Africa: get stinking rich. Use your brains. Be sharp.' I don't know what that *góra* meant, but I rem'ber the old goat's face.

We catch a train from Agra. The agent in Madras shakes his head, squirts red *pān* juice, and then laughs with dancing snake-eyes. '*Ha ji*, there's plenty diamonds and gold; lot money. You can get rich without working hard; become owner of business, have slaves, like the *Aṅgrēzī* sahibs.'

We all are frightened to be in a *jahāz* on so deep water because not one of us can swim. Each of the *jahāzis* has such a small place, if you turn you go on top of another man. Sometimes, when the wind is strong and the ship shakes like it's going to break, all pray we don't go down, down to the bottom. Times like this, the aunties don't clean the rice and *dāl*. We find sand, pieces of wood, and other rubbish mixed with the dry fish or potatoes. Then the ship smells bad after most people have vomited, shitted in a bucket even. When water to drink is not enough, we suffer extra. We have to lower a wooden bucket by rope and draw sea water to bath, in our *dhotis*. We shiver. We wash our *nitamba* with salt water. *Chī*. We'll be so ashamed if the *devtas* are watching us. If not the *pāgal samudra*, then the rotten food might kill us. Jhora *bhāī* looks at me and shakes his head, feeling bad because he can't do anything to make his fourteen-year-old brother better. One night the devil-wind howls like someone's running a catgut bow over a *sarangī* – sounds like a thousand babies crying at the same time. I close my eyes tight. Then somebody is shaking me. I awake, see it's one of the *sirdārs*. The big Sikh puts a hand round my shoulder and speaks in Hindi.

'You are Ashok Viśvās?'

'*Ji, hā.*'

'I'm so sorry, *betā*, your brother is no more.'

'What you saying, *sirdārji*?'

'He went on deck to pee – got washed 'way by big wave.'

I look at the man, my eyes and mouth wide open. Then I scream. Nobody hears. 'Jhora's in *kālā pānī*?' *Sirdārji* turns his turbaned head side to side. 'Did anyone say a prayer, do the last rites?'

'*Betā*, the *góras* don't care about all that. Only the captain worries, because he don't get paid for lost cargo.'

'But when someone dies, you have to set his soul free by cremating him and throwing the ashes in the Ganga, Jamuna...'

The head under the turban again goes from side to side. 'You contracted people were told to leave your traditions, customs, castes, and all that with the Port Officer in Madras. You can see here Brahmin, Kshatriya, like me, thrown in one big pot with *chamars*, pig eaters, and shoe makers. The sahibs know no caste; they just want donkeys...'

'You saying we was tricked when they said we can make lot money in Port Natal?'

Sirdārji's teeth shine white between his moustache and beard. 'Trick or no, it may be *sahasika*...'

'*Kyā?*'

'Adventure. You work hard and don't sit on your brain, who knows, you could become a maharaja, *ne?*'

I lift and drop my shoulders.

'You must be strong, *betā.*' He pats my head and goes. Even in the dark I could see that big Sikh's eyes shine with tears.

Drops roll down my cheeks onto my chest. I can't stop my body shaking. I look down and see something on the moving wooden floor, reach out, praying for any one of the thousands of *devtas* to turn it into food or sweetmeat, and close my fingers around it. Ha! Light as air. A boot stomps my hand. 'Ma!' It hurts.

'Stealing, huh?'

I can't speak. It's like God got angry just now and struck me dumb. Water, like the *jal* from the Ganga River, falls from my red eyes. I shake my head up and down.

'Look at me, coolie.'

I look up, see a giant white man in a funny hat, black coat with big silver buttons all the way on one side, stopping at his knees, from where thick socks go down to the side of black shoes tied with string. The *jahāzis* wear only their dirty *dhotīs*...

*

'What's *jahāzi* and *dhotī, pāpāji?*' My daughter tugs me back into the present.

'*Jahāzi* is a sailor, who instead of trousers wears a white loin cloth, called a *dhotī*, from his waist down. It is what made the white sahibs laugh and call us towel-heads, napkin-wearing camel jockeys.'

'I don't understand.'

I grin. 'You will, one day. Anyway, back to Ashok's story.'

*

The *góra* shows his yellow teeth in between black and white hairs under his nose, in his ears, and on his fat cheeks, looking like our monkey god, Hanuman.

'How old are you, boy?'

57

I don't know what the man is saying because I never learned English. So, I keep quiet.

'You travelling alone, feller?'

I suck my lips, wondering what the *mālika* of the ship means. The *góra* grabs my hand and pulls me up.

'Come with me.'

I walk behind him, like my dog, Hira, who I used to pull with a string tied to his neck. Is the man going to throw me in the sea, where *ājā* said the almighty, *paramēsvara*'s, creatures came from and where all must return, one day? Is it today for me? My eyes roll, looking everywhere. Nobody can save me. The *góra* opens the door lock with a big key, pulls me inside. *Hāi*, this is like Maharaja Jai Singh's palace, which *bāba* showed me one day in Jaipur, only smaller.

The man they call 'captain' pushes me onto a chair. I sit, frightened, the *góra* so near, his eyes the colour of the sea ... *śaitān*'s.[4] The captain bites his thin red lips, pours something from a dark green bottle into a round glass that looks like a lotus flower on a stem. It's red. *Khūn*? Is captain a Kali[5] devotee who'll drink my blood and then throw me in the *kālā pānī*, the black water what the *lascars*, the fifty Indian men who run the *jahāz*, call the Indian Ocean?

'You want a drink, boy?', Masterji asks. I'm so thirsty and hungry ... but I can't drink blood, I want ... need water. 'Go on, it's good wine ... Cabernet Sauvignon, made from grapes. I'm sorry you lost your brother overboard.'

I close my eyes tight. I am a man now, even without a *pandit* doing the *purusa diksa*.

*

Arthi pulls my forefinger. 'I know *pandit* means priest, but what is *purusa diksa?*'

'It's an initiation, a prayer done for Brahmin and Kshatriya boys when they enter manhood as teenagers. Shall I go on?' My only listener nods.

4   Satan, the devil.
5   Goddess of death, time and doomsday, often associated with sexuality and violence. But also considered to be a strong mother-figure and symbol of motherly love.

*

Sahib pours into the funny-looking glass. 'Drink up. See, it won't kill you.' He sips, makes 'aah'. I'm dying of thirst, will even drink piss. I swallow a little of the red stuff, cough. It's sour like lemon or lime. The *góra* slaps his thigh, his body shaking like he's in a trance. He sees my eyes, must be white like boiled eggs from just looking at the plate of roasted meat. I never eaten *gośt* before, my teeth make noise. I open my right hand. The brown thing falls on the table.

'Ah. You see that?' Captain points, his finger thick like a cucumber, 'It's a wine bottle stopper, made from cork...'

This man is rude... I have heard that word is English for *nūnī*.

'...cork, made from the bark of a tree, most probably from Spain.'

I try to imagine that strange country, Spain, where trees bark like dogs and they make cocks from trees? Clever, people who live there. Captain sahib takes the thing and drops it in a jug of water. Hā! It floats, like Jagesur's banana-shape fishing boat.

I'm thinking now of Jhora *bhāī*, swept 'way by a big wave made by the *paramēsvara*'s giant hand no one can see. He'd be like a tiny cork in a big jug of boiling cold water where because it's black like coal, he can see nothing. The tears come fast without sound, having seen such a lot of dead men, looking already like ghosts, skin and bones, bulging yellow eyes, sewed into bags and thrown into the sea, like rubbish, sinking like a stone. Gone! Not floating 'bout. No prayers for *atma* to take care of them and save their souls. I think if I'm not dumped in the sea and if by the grace of Saraswati I land in the place I'm supposed to go to, I can use this cork as a floater, catch some fish for supper.

The *barā* man eats like a baby, spit falling from his mouth. With his left hand ... *chī* ... he gives me a piece of *gośt*. Masterji moves both hands, like a fowl's wings, makes a sound, 'puk puk, puk puk.' I laugh. 'It's chicken, won't poison you.'

I grab what the sahib calls a drumstick and eat like Hira when he has had nothing for a week. It tastes different, not like the sour porridge, *dāl* or kedgeree, roti and tomato chutney we have in Goshukigurh. I blink; move my head sideways, a sign of happiness.

'Know where you are, boy?'

I'm eating so fast I can't talk or think of anything else. I lift and drop my shoulders.

Captain opens a long, rolled-up paper with pictures on it. He knocks on one place with a thick finger.

'Port Natal. The Enmore will land there in about eight days, around the end of August in the year of our Lord, 1874; Him and Davy Jones willing, of course.' He claps his hands, laughs like a donkey.

Hā ji! That's the place Bapū Dulelsing and Cohen sahib said we will be going, to make a fortune, whatever that is.

'Good to see you smiling, lad. We set out with 342 coolies; I'll be mightily pleased if no more are lost overboard before we drop anchor.' He hits me on my back. Something goes straight down to my stomach. I cough.

The chicken, so tasty, is finished. I suck my fingers, look up and see a big *sankha* on a cupboard that has lots of drawers.

'You like that? It called a seashell, a conch. Beautiful, isn't it? I picked it up at Goa, fourteen years ago; maybe about the time you were born.'

Captain drinks ... Cabernet Sauvignon. He pours more in my glass. Does wine make someone see beauty and colours more clearly, I wonder? Sahib gets up, brings the conch back. 'A work of art, eh?'

Ji, hā. Bhagvān's[6] handiwork, the conch, once a living being, like us. I look with wide eyes at the thing. Masterji turns his head a little and puts it to his ear.

'You can hear the sound of the sea, in here. Go on.'

I rub my hands on my dirty *dhotī*; put the *sankha* to my ear. It's true. I hear the Arabian Sea, Hind Mahasagar, the sounds of ma and *bāba*, brothers Eshwar and Rajesh, sister Radha ... This may have been made by Lord Krishna, to call the young girls or play a tune to make them sleep. Why, I'm in dreamland myself.

'...you can come here anytime you want and listen to the oceans sing and cry. It's yours. If I weren't contracted to deliver you to Hansen, I'd keep you as my cabin boy, you beautiful, stinking creature. Now, it's time for your bath.'

6   The Lord.

I blink. Captain is taking off his coat and trousers, making eyes at me. Only my mother, and some friends seen me without clothes when we bathe in the Jamuna River. But this *gora's* a good man. He took and fed me, gave me this beautiful seashell and that thing he calls a cork – for fishing. White people not like us poor Indians – they throw things away; we have nothing to give, keep everything. Captain's three times bigger 'n me, his body red, covered all over with hair. He takes my hand, pulls me into a small room where on the floor is a bath full of water, carries and puts me in there, like I'm a baby. He washes, wipes me, like ma used to. Last thing I rem'ber is his hair-full face and blue eyes.

I wake up screaming, wondering if I had a bad dream or someone on the ship was killing me. Tears flow. I see nothing in the dark, but hear the ship creaking and someone making noises like a pig. It must be *śaitān*. I see the cork and the *sankha* ... can I blow it? Will my family and friends so far away in Bharat, my *devtas*, hear and come fast to save my body and soul? Or is it only the waiting devils of the dead in the whispering sea who'll fly to this haunted *jahāz* to take me away?

*

'What happened in the captain's room, papa?'

I lick my lips, swallow. 'I don't know. The book only says my great-grandfather met *śaitān*, looking white and terrible. That's all. Must I carry on?'

Arthi frowns. 'Yes, please.'

*

I land at Port Natal and being without a father couldn't get work. But I found treasure on the *jahāz*, a shy girl named Śānti, only daughter of Arjun and Tara Misra. Her *pitāji* looks like he could eat me for supper, but the mother tells this Bengal tiger about how Jhora got washed 'way and now I have nobody; am *ākelā*. Śānti cries, and how I wish I could wipe away her tears. I sit with the Misra family breakfast and supper time. The daughter talks of life in the dusty but sometimes flooded village of Suraj in Haldia, about twenty-five miles from Calcutta. Good memory for a twelve-year-old. She tells me how her father lost their small farm because he owed moneylenders so much after getting her older sister, Indra, married. Śānti's mother smiles a lot, maybe because being a Brahmin lady she could see the future will definitely be better than the past? But will people return to their old customs and traditions, castes and religion, when they live in Port Natal? Will it be the same as Goshukigurh, only different?

Śānti and her family are taken by Mr Rick Hansen to Ottawa Estate, a sugar-cane plantation. Arjun *cācā* said I could stay with them, but the *Aṅgrēzī* sahib says no. I'm crying – will they put me in jail? What I did? Then a tall man in a turban puts a hand on my shoulder.

'*Tumhāra näm kyā, betā?*'

'Ashok.'

'Father's name and caste?'

'Viśvās, *ahir*.' A caste below the priests and warriors.[7]

The man smiles. 'Hā! You understand the meaning of your name?'

'*Nahī.*'

'In English, it means "truth and belief".' Bapū smiles, talks in Hindi to the Englishman, who looks at me and shakes his head up and down. *Sirdārji* tells me the immigration officer said I can stay with him, work on Mr Roger Puntan's sugar plantation in Springfield. 'Okay?'

I shake my head sideways. '*Ji, haiṅ.*' *Sirdār* Tika Singh will be what is called my adopted father.

Me 'n my new family worked hard on the sugar-cane field on the south bank of the Umgeni River. On Sundays we planted carrots, pumpkins, mealies, green beans, one umdoni tree and a jackfruit tree. We caught shrimps by net and fish by rods which we sold in the market. *Sirdārji* was a good man and one night, about five years afterwards when he was in a good mood and laughing too much, I think from the ganja, I told him about Śānti. The old man said nothing, but on Saturday, ma made hot water; I had a good bath and put on new clothes. We crossed the river by boat and walked to Temple Station where we caught a train to Ottawa. Then we walked on the narrow railtrack between tall sugar-cane to the cane-cutters' barracks.

---

7   A caste of cattle-herders and sometimes warriors who ruled over different parts of India and Nepal.

They were happy to see me. Śānti looked lovelier than when she was on the ship – must be 'bout seventeen years old now. *Sirdārji* and Arjun *cācā* talked into the night by the fire, drinking something I don't know. They laughed at jokes I could not understand or hear; my eyes only on the girl. What to do?

'Ashok!'

'*Bāba*?'

We are next day walking from the barracks to Ottawa village to catch the train back to Temple Station. 'Arjun said he'll be happy if you marry his daughter.'

'*Sirdārji*, I'm only nineteen years old.'

'*Ji hā*. Not a child. You gotta make babies ... boys, who must work hard, like you, *betā*.' He looks at me with raised eyebrows.

Sitting on a rock at the place we landed, after I finished my five-year indenture contract, I thought: should I go back to Goshukigurh or anywhere else in India? No, I would be like the *crores* of half-starved villagers who'll die from want, for back in those *gaons* poverty is guaranteed, life is not. Yes, rather stay here; take my chances. I made this decision when I saw a cork floating for a long time on the calm water, like a lone marigold from a cremated Hindu's wreath. I will not be alone, as long as Śānti lives by my side.

I see my floater going in and out, the line becoming tight. Hā! Something's biting. Fish for supper, for me, listening to the ocean and faraway people and places, the conch whose whispers cut like a knife through the darkest night and bring some comfort to a lost soul, a lone cork, bobbing on a vast and restless sea, no diamonds or gold in sight.

*

I close the diary; a tear falls on it. For a moment I sit silent, head thrust forward as if I'm looking for the ancestors to emerge out of the gloom as new immigrants. Not possible – coolies are not welcome, even as third-class citizens. *Pardādā* could've been a writer if he was not destined to be a cane-cutter, a turban and *dhotī*-attired slave. Karma.

I look beside me; Arthi is asleep. So much for my storytelling ability: a cure for insomnia. Dee's saxophone is soothing. I must have a drink and go to the dance-floor, try the Twist, practise what I've learned at Runga Naidoo's Ballroom Dancing Studio. Wish Asha was here as my partner, rather than looking down with my forefathers upon a grown man weeping. Someone is impersonating Roy Orbison, singing *Only the Lonely*. But I haven't sent in a request, nor am I lonely as I look at little Sleeping Beauty beside me.

In the shade of the umdoni tree under the watchful old eyes of *ājī*, ma would singe the wool 'n hair of sheep's head 'n trotters with a glowing hot tyre iron. The smell of piss and burning shit pervades. But the curry in sugar-beans is aromatic and tasty, as is the boiled-then-fried tongue 'n brains. Ma would slit the throat of a Zulu fowl and collect the blood in an enamel bowl and immediately fry it. She would also clean fowl's head 'n feet here, but nowadays I don't eat these, not with separated toothless jaws, black eyes drowned in gunpowdered gravy, pleading then screaming 'Don't eat me!' In my earlier days, I had two choices: eat or starve. Today I wouldn't touch such stuff, or a sacrificial goat's balls, even when *dronk*. Posh food for some droolers. Am I a kind of gourmand, a glutton or a gourmet, a *pētū*, someone who appreciates good food? Ma asked me once only.

'Why must you drink before supper every night, Rohit?'

'Surely you don't expect me to eat your cooking when sober, ma?'

In the sitting room on one wall is a sepia-toned framed oval picture of *ājā* and *ājī* looking like they see a ghost coming out from under the black cloth over the photographer's head. Grandfather sports a white turban while granny has the end of her sari draped over her head. In another black 'n white photo, ma sits on a Globe chair showing teeth, while *bāba* stands beside her looking like he needs to use the lavatory, pronto. The only colour photos are one of Arthi on my lap trying to blow out the candle at her first birthday party, and another taken at age five, showing a remarkable resemblance to her mother. My daughter has her ma's genes, thank god not my tattered ones. Hope she didn't inherit my simple brain.

My family property is a lot to lose unless I settle with that Jew-Scotsman, Campbell ... fast. The *gōra* is gonna foreclose, whatever that means, because I'm owing Natal Building Society £18,000. I can't believe it! *Bāba* inherited a small house from his father, renovated it with a Durban Corporation loan, paid off in ten years, got the title deed. The first Coronation clay brick 'n tile house in the district, with meranti tongue 'n groove floor three feet above the dark and mysterious cellar ... a 'mansion' sitting proud on a hill, with a view of Blue Lagoon. My great-grandfather and the people he came with from India worked like slaves, left us something, at least. All over India, poor workers in life-long enslavement to the Thakurs,[8] shedding sweat, tears, and blood, for a small plate of little food. Same here, in Natal. Our mind is also trapped in our numb skull, making us think we're creatures of the *gōra*. Kismet? Naw. We're fools to believe we can't design our own destiny.

But now, I have only me to blame, lying in a dark hole with a bottle of Mainstay cane spirit and my ganja pipe ... for eight years, since beautiful Asha was snatched from me. Ours was a love marriage, would you believe, in 1953? Got fired from the police force for killing a pickpocket who took my *patnī's* life. Karma? No, Rohit Viśvās, Ashok's great-grandson, 'though I'm nowhere near 'great'. Thinking of the story I told my daughter, I realise what's past is history. It's funny, but you forget what you would like to rem'ber, and rem'ber what you'd rather forget. I must unravel the mystery of our bondage, break the shackles, or endure an everlasting death. I'm a private detective, aren't I, the first in Durban, perhaps the only one in Africa? Get on with the job, man. The shrill ring of the phone jolts me out of my daytime nightmare.

I learned that my mother's father came to South Africa in 1886, not because he heard 'bout the discovery of gold on the Witwatersrand. He worked as a coalminer in different parts of Natal, married late, and settled as a cane-worker at Ottawa.

Like Arjun *cācā's* house, *nānā's* was made of ash blocks, bag-washed and painted white. The corrugated iron roof was held down by big blue pumpkins, taken down when yellow, and fried with onions, dried mustard seed, red chillies, and brown sugar. Yummy? The floors were hand-plastered with dung. Holy cow! The barracks had two dark 'bedrooms', twelve feet from the small,

8   Title used for landlord in several Indian and Nepalese princely states.

smoke-blackened kitchen, next to which was a tiny 'bathroom' where you would 'shower' on Sunday by pouring water from a twenty-five-gallon Laurel paraffin container over your head, using a jam tin. The barrackers used a public lavatory, four room each for men and women. The cold concrete slab seat had a hole over an open galvanised iron bucket above which frenzied green flies hovered in excitement. Even with this racket, you sometimes heard the plop when a lump hits the shit surface.

Depending on her mood and the number of visitors, *nanī* would sacrifice a duck, grown plump from swallowing muck floating in the open drains. I'm allergic to duck curry; goat's not bad.

Nānā and *nanī* started work in the dark, six in the morning, hoeing between the rows of sugar-cane, until two or four. Grandfather would sit on a bench in the sun, bare feet on a wooden stool, white turban removed to show close-cropped salt 'n pepper hair, with trademark beard and handlebar moustache. He'd 'savour' a large chipped enamel cup of sour porridge, same fare as breakfast. After a burp or three, he'd take the *chīllum* I fetched for him, fill and tamp the ganja, then light it, sucking with cheeks hollowed. What a life!

I shiver, not from cold. We're already in the Kalyug, Kali's Age of Destruction. I fear things will get worse for us coolies as the Brits and the Dutchmen combine forces to suppress us battlers, when South Africa becomes a republic in five months' time, on 31 May 1961.

Back to India? But we've burned our boats, and all.

*

Glossary of Hindi (North Indian) terms

ājā	paternal grandfather
ājī	paternal grandmother
ākelā	alone, lonely
Aṅgrēzī	English language, Englishman
atma	god
bāba	father or respected elder
baiṅgan	eggplant; aubergine; brinjal
bapū/bapūji	respected form of address to a high caste/ class elder
barā	big; large; hefty man or woman
betā/betī	son/daughter
bhāī	brother; respected form of address to an older male
cācā/cācāji	uncle (respectful form of address); paternal uncle
chī	expression of disgust, equivalent to *sies*
chīllum	wooden pipe for smoking marijuana
crore	ten million
dādā/pardādā	paternal grandfather/great-grandfather
dāl	lentils; soup made of lentil(s)
devta	Hindu god/deity
dharoo	alcohol; alcoholic drink
dhotī	loin cloth worn by men and boys
ganja	Indian hemp, marijuana, dagga
góra	white or European male; light-skinned Indian male
gośt	meat
hā/hā ji/ji hā	yes; yes indeed
hāi	expression of surprise, sigh
hirē	diamond
hookah	curved pipe for smoking tobacco or marijuana
jahāz/i	ship/sailor
jal	drop of water; nectar; water from Ganges River
ji	yes; respectful way of addressing someone, attached to name
kahānī/kīsa	story
kālā/kālā pānī	black; black water (the Indian Ocean)
khūn	blood

67

kisa	story
kyā	what?
lascar	Asian sailor
mālika/mālikin	boss; supervisor (male/female)
nahī	no
ne	isn't that so?
nitamba	bum; arse; buttock
nūnī	penis
pān	betel leaf (like *khat*), eaten with *supari* – betel nut
pāgal	madness; insane person
pāpā/pāpāji	father
paramēsvara	God; The Almighty
patnī	wife
pitāji	father
roti	hand-made unleavened mealie meal or cake flour bread
sahasika	adventure
sahib/sahiba	respectful address to a superior man/woman
samudra	sea, ocean
sankha	conch, seashell
sarangi	home-made fiddle carved out of a tree trunk or gourd
sirdār/sirdārji	overseer; foreman
sona	gold

india has left us

Eddie Bruce-Jones

(for ali b)

india has left us
in this place
smitten with the distance
of an arm's length
and two soles and palms
laboured of their brown rivulets
leaving roads and rivers etched
back through the powder
whole cartographies savaged
each time we press
the wet mound of atta[1]
we dust our hands so it will not
stick around
to texture the wood
or fill in the space
between the digits,
the heady remembered
lifted into
salty ashen plumes

and so
a map is always orphaned
on the flame
and swallowed by the crisp
of the rising roti

1   Wheat flour.

india has left us
alive with a cumin tongue
parched between leafy halves
edged of tattered urdu
clamped beneath a tiny vessel
bronze and mounted
ivory shingles
ashen insides:
tastes
like all the pots, stored away
in cupboards fragranced
by the dead of pepper
seeds for the sapling deciduous
trees harvested somewhere
close to here

in each room
of each house
of metal and wood
an urn
an elephant
three bronze lanterns
long gone cold
on some kitchen window ledge
a riddled hanuman watches us
silently peeling skin
into sacred dust

Chutney Love

Gabrielle Jamela Hosein

Dem call meh Chutney Love
And if yuh see meh belly roll
Man cyan stop meh on a stage
When de chutney take control

I eh nobody bowjie[1]
No promised doolahin[2]
But when de tassa[3] start to roll up
Beta, dem lyrics yuh have
I done write myself in

Ah could speak a lil Hindi
From meh nani and Indian movie
Dem does lick up meh curry and roti
An, well, meh house does see
Both Eid and Diwali
But dis chutney I does feel it
Curving in all meh wrist an ankle bone
Ah hundred and fifty years we woman singing it
An not in matikor[4] alone

I never yet did leave Trinidad
Since India was left on de boats
So I know dis chutney is real Trini make
National culture like calypso
We did sing it

1   Sister-in-law.
2   Indian bride.
3   Drums.
4   A female ritual ceremony that takes place the night before a wedding begins.

We did dance it
From back all dem years come through
Yuh think we was quiet and obedient
An dis wining ting is new
When dem young village gyuls was at a wedding
Meh nani coulda show dem a ting or two

Now some ah dem doh like dis chutney
Say how we does get on too wild
But is de freedom in we spirit that give chutney
Its pride and style
And look how now we everywhere
Soca show, radio, parang⁵ and carnival
Sitar, tabla, Hindi and Indian history
Claiming a place in Trini bacchanal

Now I eh have much learning eh
No big, big book
No fancy word
But is in we music, we music
Dat de lesson can be heard
In carnival last season
After we struggle a hundred an fifty years for recognition
Not just Indian but African singing chutney
And in Hindi
As jahaji bhai I hear dem say we coming together
Jes doh forget meh jahaji bahen if yuh please

---

5   Trinidadian musical genre that is sung in Spanish.

Now one last last, last ting before I go bout how
Indians and Africans does fight an buse each other so
Is one set ah noise for a lil political power
But we both cross water for empire
And ever since we lan up here together
Is with only one history that we grow
Now I watching all kinda people feel we music for so
An everybody coming to see that we was one people
From since long ago

So when ah tell yuh I love de chutney
For how much we have achieved
Ah want to see yuh belly roll
And gyul
Play up yuhself
Fuh real

Brotherhood of the Boat:
Fijians and Football in North America

Akhtar Mohammed

When I was a child, on every September long weekend, my father Taj Mohammed would wake my older brother Zafar and me around 7 am for an early breakfast. My dad would put on his cap, his favourite trousers, short-sleeve dress-shirt, watch and a generous amount of cologne. We would load our station wagon with footballs, trophies and folders of papers and drive from our suburb in the Greater Vancouver Area to the football field.

We arrived around 7.30 am at the South Surrey Athletic Park, which was located only five minutes north of the Pacific Ocean. The Sunnyside Acres forest surrounded the area; due to this the air was crisp and fresh. A few other vehicles were already in the parking lot and a white tent was being set up by an older cousin of ours, who was the owner of a tenting company. The two tents were placed a safe distance from one of the six fields being used this weekend, to serve as a safe space from which to administer the tournament. In the meantime, my brother and I worked together to unload a number of trophies from the trunk of the station wagon. We were especially careful with the tournament's prize trophy. Both of us held it to ensure its safety. During one of the organising meetings held at our house late into the summer night we had overheard that parts of it had been constructed in Italy and it was worth $3000. We arranged the trophies from largest to smallest reading each description, while debating who we thought would win each respective award: Most Valuable Player, Golden Boot, Best Defender, Best Midfield, Best Rookie, Sportsmanship Award, Best Goalie and Best Dressed Team.

Slowly the caravans of vehicles carrying the teams and their supporters arrived bearing the license plates of their respective areas. We waited for the cursive red 'California' license plates to see their new star players. The California players exited their vehicles bearing their best pre-game attire, which was a mix of athletic and hip-hop gear. Our Indian-Fijian brethren from California intimidated us. They fully embraced hip-hop culture and this lent them an air of mystique. They were located on the west coast, home to some of

74

the best hip-hop artists in the world; we naturally perceived their understanding of the genre to be more authentic than ours.

The nets would be placed on six of the fields with all boundaries relined to lessen debates among the players and linesmen. Most importantly, the food tent would be prepared. The meat supplier would arrive with Halal chicken burgers and vegetarian options to serve the multireligious requirements of the community. My mother Hamshira and my two elder sisters, Tasneem and Nasreen, would arrive later, bringing anything that we had forgotten and to help with the administration of the tournament over the weekend. Soon afterwards the brave referees would arrive. The lead referee Mike would begin by outlining the key issues to look out for. One small request the referees would make was to ask for the organiser's support in ensuring the crowds did not interfere with the linesmen's view of the outlines. Over a thousand fans would be expected to watch the finals and historically the passion of the crowd often impeded the linesmen's duties. With tension increasing as the tournament progressed, the perennial problem was how to protect the referees from the players. I remember Mike very well. Known in my family as 'the referee', he was instrumental in convincing my dad to sign my brother and me for the local football club, Surrey United, after noticing our potential talent when we played at the edge of the field.

By 8.30 am almost all of the sixteen teams from across North America had arrived. It was time for the opening ceremonies of the fifteenth edition of the tournament to begin. On this particular long weekend in September 1997, I had sat in front of the television with my family the night prior to the tournament and learned of the passing of Princess Diana. I had never heard much about her at school in Canada, but my parents were in tears that night. I didn't understand why they were so upset. Only later did I learn that my parents' country, the one they had grown up in, was a British colony until 1970. They felt connected to the British monarchy in a way that I did not understand then.

The next morning my dad took the microphone and began his opening remarks with a tribute to Princess Diana. He asked the teams and fans to observe a minute's silence, which was followed by a Scottish bagpipe performance to mark the beginning of the tournament. My father continued as normal by naming the sixteen lined-up teams, and as he called out each name the goalie standing at the head of that team waved in acknowledgement. The teams included: Combine (Vancouver), Flagstaff (California), Delta Stars, Tanoa, Sacramento Combine, and of course the Richmond Rangers. In Ivor Evans, the latter had the star player of the tournament who was the pride of the community. He had formerly represented Fiji's national team and was currently the star player for the Vancouver 86er's, a professional team in the North American Soccer League. Evans, of indigenous Fijian descent, was a passionate player to say the least. He possessed a stocky frame and often put on performances of his dribbling skills. Evans was one of my favourite players as a child, perhaps because he was one of the best I've ever seen.

The participating teams were not newly formed in Vancouver and California, but were the result of the Fijians transplanting their football clubs from their homeland to their respective new countries. The clubs maintained the same names, logos and uniforms. Indian football in Fiji began when it was taught at the Marist Brothers Indian School in Toorak, Suva. The students later organised coordinated social games that would mark the beginning of the club system. The Indian Reform League was founded in 1924, four years after the indenture system ended, by a group of educated Indian-Fijians, many of whom were Christians. Prior to creating the league, the group had asked the Suva YMCA if it could use their facilities, but was denied as the organisation did not admit Indians at the time. By 1927 the league had organised a tournament for Suva-based schools at Albert Park. It included the Methodist Mission School, Marist Brothers School, Munivatu Indian School and Islamia School. As the Colonial Sugar Refining Company (CSR) teams and Suva-based teams gained in popularity, a Suva businessman Arthur Stanley Farebrother worked with the leaders of the respective teams from Suva, Rewa, Ba, Levuka and Lautoka to establish the Fiji Indian Football Association, on 8 October 1938. It took another five months for the constitution to be written, and it was finally adopted with the approval of all members on 22 April 1939. The association organised the inter-district competition (IDC), which provided a platform for regional rivalry between urban and rural areas of the country. In 1961 it was decided that the association would remove the word 'Indian' from the title in order to gain acceptance from the Fédération Internationale de Football Association (FIFA). This would acknowledge that the team on the pitch reflected the diversity of an increasingly multicultural society. The greatest beneficiary of this policy was Ba Football Association, as they won the IDC tournament five times with the support of many indigenous Fijian players. The utopian ideals of a multicultural Fiji did not come to fruition, but those who came to form the diaspora were able to build upon the foundations established on their island.

By 9 am all six fields were occupied by teams battling through the attrition of the round-robin stage of the tournament. Most teams had to finish in the top two of their respective division to make it to the next round. Not all of the fans had arrived yet, but there were now enough kids to play a children's game on the side. Although the sizing up of talent was conducted during the opening ceremonies involving the competing teams, the unofficial children's game was no less intense. With no formal rules, no uniform, no established reputation and no scouting report available on our opponents, we had no idea how good these 'California kids' were. After a few games and earning some mutual respect, we exchanged names: 'Nicholas', 'Rajesh, 'Irshaad'. The annual tournament was the only time I would see some some of these children; those of us closer to home were to watch each other rise, over the next ten years, through the ranks of the local and provincial teams to become key players on the adult men's teams.

By lunchtime, we would attempt to gather enough money from our parents to get our hands on burgers. The meat requirements of each community would be adhered to. No pork for the Muslims, no beef for the Hindus; it was typically not an issue. Christian, Hindu or Muslim, all were the same, all Fijian. The purpose was to get everyone together for the annual tournament. If we focused on our differences, we would never be able to celebrate the football ability of our community. We were all the shades and religions of the subcontinent: Sikh, Hindu, Muslim and Christian, with our Indigenous Fijian superstar Ivor Evans, a couple of Chinese Fijians, and European Canadians who played as 'imports'. For the Fijian diaspora in North America, the strong bonds and social levelling that emerged on the pitch mirrored the formation of the early bonds created by the indentured Indian-Fijian community, across caste and religion. For us as a diaspora community of Fijians, the football pitch became the ultimate equaliser where effort, ability and passion would be the only measure of your worth.

My family's history in Fiji began on 24 March 1894, with the migration of my maternal great-grandfather Juman Khan, son of Din Mohamed. He was a Pashtun from Kanpur, Uttar Pradesh, who left the subcontinent in the aftermath of the collapse of the Mughal Empire and the establishment the British Raj; Fiji would become home for his descendants for almost eighty years. When the Second World War extended into the Pacific, where the Americans and the Allies fought against Imperial Japan, my maternal grandfather Mohammed Razak Khan was enlisted as a soldier and fought for the cause of 'democracy' and 'equality' under the Union Jack banner. He received half the pay of his European compatriots. After the war he returned home to Fiji to continue his work at the public works department where he remained until retirement. Mohammed and his wife, Khairul Nisha raised thirteen children in Suva. His children attended British schools, played for their local football clubs, participated in civic society and contributed to a multicultural society. Yet from 1970, following Fiji's independence from Britain, life was disrupted on multiple occasions as the country became divided by ethnic tensions. This conflict between Indian-Fijians and Indigenous-Fijians, caused the migration of close to 250,000 Indian-Fijians and led to subsequent economic recession and a bloody coup d'état after the election of the country's first prime minister of Indian origin, Mahendra Chaudhry.

The Fijian Indians of North America and its larger community have organised the North American Fijian Soccer Association tournament successfully for the past thirty-five years, with competitive Fijian Indian leagues in Vancouver and California and amateur teams all along the west coast and Canada. Our community has almost no connection with India and increasingly little with Fiji. We have been twice displaced and, as a consequence, Fiji has become almost as foreign to me as India is to my parents. Both in Fiji and in North America the community of descendants of indentured labourers have reconstituted and rebuilt their lives in the face of immense pressure, but with little complaint against the British or Fijian governments. There is almost no reference to the indenture system any more, yet we still live by the *jahaji bhai* sentiment (brotherhood of the boat). We remain open to others, we move forward to make our lives better and we don't restrict ourselves solely to our Indian heritage since it does not adequately explain how much our culture has grown.

The tournament would end with a late-afternoon final on Sunday, with tension rising to its highest levels because the competing teams were the best team from Vancouver pitted against the best from California. At this point my brother and I would begin walking around the field to pick up the rubbish and the burgers would be selling at a discounted price to ensure that everything went. Hungry players would eagerly try to get a few free ones. The referees would be huddled behind the administrative staff to keep a safe distance from any players holding grievances. The closing ceremonies would begin. The tension at this point of the day had less to do with competitive spirit and more to do with ego. Who would earn the Most Valuable Player trophy? Who would win Best Goalie, Best Defender, Best Midfielder, Best Rookie? Typically, emotion would overtake logic, and an unsung hero, who performed better than expected in the finals, would take the Most Valuable Player trophy over the outright superstar, who everyone knew was by far the best player. The unspoken methodology of the selection process would often leave a few players perpetually unhappy, a grudge that would be held until the next tournament.

The sixteen-team tournament, which featured official letters of recognition from local mayors, the provincial premier and even the prime minister, was the manifestation of the collective skills gained by the descendants of indentured labourers since SS *Leonidas* left Calcutta on 3 March 1879, and arrived in Levuka, Fiji on 14 May 1879. Yet the indenture system, which lasted from 1879 to 1916 and transported 60,000 Indians to Fiji, has never defined this community or limited its ambitions. I'm sure those first few to step foot on the SS *Leonidas* never imagined that their great-grandchildren would become formidable football players, with organised leagues and international tournaments. I'm sure the British didn't either. We exist, as a periphery among the periphery, but quite content with that, always moving forward and forever united by football.

The Heist[1]

Deirdre Jonklaas Cadiramen

Perian, a man of indeterminate age, was the *tappal* coolie, whose duty it was to take the mailbag to and from the local post office for the isolated hill-country tea estate. Dark leathery wizened skin, the veins of his scrawny bowlegs protruding like knotted cord as if to escape their prison, slight frame, stooped after years of carrying heavy canvas mailbags on his back while trekking along winding uphill roads. Fiercely independent, his rejection of progress was vociferous: he had no need of a new bicycle offered by Ron, the estate superintendent. His legs had not betrayed him in two decades, walking around ten miles each way daily (barring weekends) from his living quarters in a line-room on the estate to the post office in Passara town and back.

*

Ron, the estate superintendent, and his wife Nadine planned to celebrate their wedding anniversary in style. Their ten years on a remote upcountry tea estate in the Uva district had at times been lonely and monotonous except for 'club days', tournaments and social occasions at the planters' Passara Gun Club where two World War Two cannons stood at either end of the verandah. The Uva Club in Badulla held similar events, and there were biweekly English movies at the cinema in Passara town and occasional dinner invitations.

Their guest list of forty included eight house guests arriving from Colombo, 166 miles away. Also invited were planters from neighbouring estates in Passara within a radius of eleven miles, accustomed to night driving for social occasions, measuring distance by time taken. Bachelors in planting circles outnumbered females, so when tipplers gravitated towards the bar, others evened out as dance partners.

One item on Nadine's checklist was unticked: tomatoes. Cook's reason for what ailed their tomato patch was inconsequential. What

---

1 Part of this piece was published under the title 'The True Story of the Heist', in Deirdre Jonklaas Cadiramen, *Jigsaw* (Bay Owl Press, Colombo, 2009).

irked her was that the menu would be imperfect without fresh, ripe tomatoes. Her keen sense of social importance, afforded by Ron's position, made her snobbish and pretentious in an inoffensive way, at times bordering on the ludicrous, taking pains to do things in a classy style to impress.

Ron arranged for five kilos of quality tomatoes from the cooler climes of Nuwara Eliya to be transported seventy-six miles by rail.

Delivery of the tomatoes coincided with that month's pay, so the *tappal* coolie would be driven twenty-one miles in the estate car to Badulla to collect the tomatoes from the railway station, while Ron went to collect the coolie pay from the agency office, which had to be done by someone in authority – the superintendent himself, no less. For this vital mission, Muttiah the watchman, armed with his shotgun, would act as a one-man security force.

*

Karthelis, the driver, stopped the Morris Minor Traveller under the porch and got out. The scar of a knife-wound cutting through his right eyebrow gave him a quizzical expression. He wore a white sarong, belted, shirt unbuttoned with sleeves rolled up, displaying prominent tattoos of a snake and an anchor on each of his muscular arms.

Muttiah, wearing a brown-checked sarong and khaki hangout shirt, walked up the driveway carrying his shotgun on his ample shoulder, its butt resting in the grip of an outsize palm.

Perian followed with empty mailbag, also wearing a brown-checked sarong, khaki sleeveless coat with rows of pockets down the front, upturned collar hanging loosely over a faded crumpled shirt.

Perian and Muttiah were plantation Tamils, possibly fourth-generation descendants of indentured labourers brought by the British from South India at the beginning of the nineteenth century, to work on tea, coffee, rubber and coconut plantations. Some had arrived alone, others with families. The women worked as tea-pluckers, each paid according to the weight of tea gathered, and other labourers were paid an hourly rate. Gangs of estate workers were supervised by overseers, who were managed by a head overseer. Each family, with as many as ten children, lived in one line-room within a row of twelve, and everyone used common toilets and a common tap where men and women washed out in the open – since the lack of a nearby waterfall meant no spouts could be installed. Their sick were attended to in dispensaries on the estate, manned by dispensers providing basic free medicine for simple illnesses. Their children received free education in schools on the estate up to the fourth or fifth standard in core subjects like reading, writing and arithmetic.

Bareheaded and barefoot, the trio's respectful salutation to Nadine was acknowledged with a slight inclination of her head.

Wearing khaki shorts, planter's check shirt and walking shoes, since his field-and-factory visits earlier in the morning, Ron sat in the front passenger seat with Karthelis at the wheel. Muttiah sat behind, the butt of his gun on the floorboards. Perian sat beside him, the mailbag across his knees.

Accustomed to each other's company on uneventful runs each month, they sat silent on the return journey; the car driven at a steady pace, skillfully negotiating hairpin bends on the upward climb of a deserted road. Approaching a flat, straight surface at the summit, Karthelis increased speed. Passing a stretch of jungle on either side they reached a culvert under a bend. A waterfall trickled between boulders from highland on their left, flowing under the culvert into a stream through lowland to their right.

Much less tiring than when I used to be driven to Colombo every month to withdraw coolie pay from a bank, mused Ron until his thoughts were interrupted by a sound like a pistol shot ripped through the air, destroying their shared tranquility.

A crack in the middle of the windscreen resembled a spider's web, the grooves on either side of it gradually extending to both extremities. Karthelis slammed the brakes. The car ground to a screeching halt, jolting the passengers.

'What's that?', asked Muttiah.

'Maybe falling fruit', replied Karthelis.

'But there aren't remnants of pulp', said Ron.

'Maybe struck by a bird in flight', suggested Karthelis.

'There are no traces of feathers or blood.'

'I'll go check, Master Sir.'

Karthelis got out and examined the damage. Muttiah looked from his window and pointed to a stone the size of a lemon near the left front tyre. Karthelis surveyed parasitic creepers on overhead branches, wondering if an errant monkey was the culprit.

Before this could be verified, four men, bare-bodied but for loincloths, their faces masked with black-cloth-folded-into-triangles from below their eyes down to their necks, sprang from under the culvert and surrounded them. Their brown bodies, oiled so they could easily slip out of someone's grasp if caught, glistened under the harsh sunlight.

An assailant pointed a pistol at Karthelis, as if to take aim between his eyes.

An accomplice pulled Ron out of the car, tied his hands to the sides of his body, winding the long rope twice round, pulled him to the side of the road and tied him to a jak tree, before blindfolding him and tying his feet. Ron's tanned features showed his aggravation; the droop of his broad shoulders and lowered head took a few inches from his full height. He clenched and unclenched his fists, seething with resentment at his helplessness, his chest close to bursting under the strain of flooding emotions.

Another ruffian pushed the front seat down, grappled with Muttiah and dragged him out, giving him no chance to flip the safety-catch of his shotgun, and after a tussle snatched the gun from Muttiah. He blindfolded his quarry with a grimy cloth, tied his hands and feet with rope and shoved him aside with his foot. A vein protruding from the skin on Muttiah's forehead unconsciously displayed his frustration as he lay on the road, half under the car, shoulder muscles taut, blood rapidly coursing through his veins, his head pounding with unuttered curses.

Karthelis, dragged to the car and shoved in his seat, had no chance of retaliation, with a revolver pressed against his neck, blindfold, his hands tied to the steering wheel, and his feet tied together. The car keys were wrenched from the ignition and thrown into the stream. He ground his teeth in fury.

As the fourth approached Perian, he cried, 'Oh my god!' and flung his sweat-drenched body on the seat, shielding his face with his hands. Nerves aquiver with multitudinous anticipated terrors, he sensed rather than saw the door open and the removal of the sack beside him. His body shuddered involuntarily as a clenched fist boxed his head, momentarily stunning him.

The victims heard an engine running and guessed it belonged to the getaway car. Its doors grated open and slammed shut, the engine revved, followed by the crash of gears and the screech of tyres.

Perian raised a trembling hand and lowered Karthelis' blindfold from behind, then pulled out a penknife from one of his many shirt-pockets, leant towards Karthelis and cut the rope tying his hands. Karthelis opened the cubby-hole, removed a penknife, and cut the bonds binding his own feet. He then freed Muttiah and together they unbound Ron.

Their search for the car keys proved futile.

*

Late morning turned into afternoon, afternoon into evening, evening into night.

Perian flung himself onto the seat, muttering incoherently.

*

At the sound of an approaching lorry, Karthelis and Muttiah jumped in the middle of the road to flag it down, waving their hands frantically above their heads. The lorry halted, its headlights on. The driver's bloodshot eyes, unshaven visage and slurred speech were telltale signs of exhausting hours at the wheel, yet these did not hinder him from engaging in a logical discussion of their problem.

The lorry driver asked them to get into their vehicle. He produced two lengths of wire and, after several attempts, established contact with the circuit under the dashboard and cranked the starter. The engine spluttered and came alive. Ron, Karthelis and Muttiah waved their thanks, before driving off. Perian, lying down with his face on the seat, was oblivious to the coolies, trudging in the dark without torch or lantern and starting to run to cover as much distance as possible in the time that the car's headlamp beams lit their path.

As they rounded the last bend leading uphill to the bungalow driveway, each started at the false gaiety which greeted their arrival, along with noise of generator and brightness of every light in bungalow and garden, despite the late hour.

Nadine, leaning against the door frame looked ashen, in high-heeled mules, quilted-satin housecoat, her hair restrained in a plait. The bungalow staff stood deferentially, a few paces behind, silent as usual, barefoot, still in white livery, expecting to serve drinks on the lawn, followed by dinner in the dining room and coffee in the lounge.

The grating of the gramophone winding down passed unheeded, despite its needle scratching the record and slowing down with each revolution, distorting the melody, until it got stuck in a groove and made a hideous sound.

Ron turned to help Perian from the car and was alarmed to find him seated with his sarong hitched up to his chest, clutching his stomach.

I didn't think he was injured, he thought, feeling guilty.

Perian emerged stiffly, unable to straighten, yet asserting his independence by shaking off helping hands.

He prostrated himself at Ron's feet, releasing the front of his sarong, which unwound and crumpled on the ground. Gaudy chintz shorts worn underneath held it up at the sides and back. With a clink of coins and rustle of notes, a sack fell in front of him.

Ron picked it up, realising the thieves had missed their target and mistakenly made off with the sack of tomatoes. Its contents intact, he locked the sack in the iron safe camouflaged by a life-size portrait of his great-grandmother.

Perian was thumped on the shoulder, patted on the back, poured a warm beverage, led into the kitchen and seated in front of the fully stoked Dover stove. As if in a trance, he tapped his forehead with his free hand between sips.

Karthelis and Muttiah satisfied the curiosity of the bungalow staff who were plying them with food and asking a salvo of questions; they were in no hurry to retire to their line-rooms.

Ron phoned the police station and asked for the inspector. The duty constable didn't need to ask who was calling or to be asked to transfer the call to the inspector's house: relationships between the local police and estate management had always been cordial. Ron told him what had happened and said that since the coolie pay was safe, the investigation process could wait until morning. He smiled grimly, thinking that if the phone lines weren't working, he'd have had to wait until first light to send a labourer running downhill to the main road and hitch a lift from a carter or a cyclist, to deliver his message to the police station.

Muttiah took a kerosene lantern and set off for his nightwatch. Within minutes nine strikes on his gong was heard throughout the estate, denoting the time and providing an assurance that he was on his rounds.

Perian took a coconut shell with an oilwick in its middle. Karthelis preferred a flame-torch – a stick with a cloth dipped in kerosene tied round the end and set alight – to keep away serpents and wild boar. As they neared the inky blackness of the line-rooms, a dog emerged from each room, barking to alert the owners. Routinely retiring for the night at six o'clock, the families were disturbed from their sleep and came out to check. Once again, Perian and Karthelis related their ordeal.

Nothing ever deterred the tea pluckers from their usual dawn start for the day's work, so the previous day's news was relayed at a speed of knots, spreading from the estate to the village in double-quick time. It transpired that villagers had seen thugs from a neighbouring village in the vicinity the previous day. The labourers informed their honorary head responsible for estate labourers – like a welfare officer or a village headman – who told the chief clerk, who told the assistant superintendent, who told the superintendent (Ron), who told the inspector, who told his counterpart in the neighbouring village; the culprits were traced and arrested.

With no opportunity to replenish the stolen tomatoes, now evidence rotting in police custody, Nadine had no option but to manage without them.

The hold-up spot came to be referred to in the vernacular by labourers and villagers alike as 'Tomato Bend'.

Buckets

Stella Chong Sing

Maybe we've forgotten
the crossing
because we weren't there

but in dreams we visit you,
see the wet boards
under your feet,
leave the swaying doubts
to the ship's master

Maybe we've forgotten
the rough outline of
versions of
Victorian buildings
while scuttling in line
to the strange sounds of
fortune-teller birds
laughing above

Maybe we've forgotten
how language barriers
changed your names
to our names,
yet they carry on
a legacy

Maybe we've forgotten
how the scale
tipped
not always in your favour

Maybe we've forgotten
the buckets

Have we forgotten
the toiling of hope,
how the sun really feels
when dreams are
put in reverse?

I have not forgotten
the stories of Ajee,[1]
born on a boat
between lost lands
who persevered
even after
watching her three sons
pass before their time

I have not forgotten
the woman
who carried buckets
of dirt for pennies
to send her children
to school,
who fell in love
twice,
once arranged
and once destined
to a man and not
the colour of his skin

---

1   Paternal grandmother.

I have not forgotten
this woman
who appears in
my dreams
holding buckets
in hands
that did not
forget to live

The Tamarind Tree

Brij V. Lal

Jala hai jism jahan dil bhi jal gaya hoga
Kuraidtey ho jo ab raakh justju kya hai

If the body is burnt, so must have been the heart
Why rake the ashes now, what is the search for?

Ghalib

May 1962. The Tamarind Tree was struck by lightning and razed. Father cried inconsolably. His indentured father had died a few weeks earlier, and now the Tree was gone. We children had no idea about the cause or the depth of his grief. It was not until many decades later that I discovered through a circuitous route of conjectures, assumptions and reflections that the Tamarind Tree ground was *terra sacra* for Father, a place of special memories linking him to another past and time. Father was not much of a talker, parsimonious with his emotions like most men of his generation, except when angry. Our conversations, if any, were perfunctory, more in the nature of brisk instructions from him about household chores to be completed before and after school. But that sight of a grown-up man crying like a child remained with me through all my many long years of research and writing about our past. I can still recall Father's tattered, wet khaki clothes clinging to his body as he stood in the drenching rain in the middle of the compound muttering words of loss and regret which I have now forgotten. I picture him having his head shaved and his usually well-tended, luxuriant moustache permanently reduced to a stubble, as is customary following bereavement, and the village old-timers gathering at our place for a week-long period of *Ramayana* recital[1] and devotional singing, all ending in a communal vegetarian feast. The details would well up whenever the subject of indenture arose.

---

1 The ancient Hindu epic poem, which was especially significant for indentured labourers because the majority of them came from Uttar Pradesh, where this 'exile' narrative is set. The regular performances they held would have preserved this knowledge for subsequent generations.

The Tamarind Tree was on the banks of the Wailevu River, about a mile down the hill from the headquarters of Labasa's Tua Tua Sector Office of the Colonial Sugar Refining Company (CSR), the main employer of Indian indentured labour in Fiji. My very vague memory is of a tall, gnarled tree, vine-wrapped, standing forlornly in overgrown grass, abandoned. But I saw it when its glory days as the *adda* (the gathering place) of the *girmitiyas* (descendants of indentured labourers) had long been over. For Father, it was different. The Tree had been there for as long as he could remember. It took him back to his own childhood in the immediate post-indenture days of the 1920s. How the Tree came to Tua Tua no one really knew. People said it was brought by the early girmitiyas sometime in the mid 1890s when cane came to Labasa. Others thought it arrived much later with the South Indians. Tamarind is an essential ingredient in many South Indian dishes. But the question of origin was moot now. Who brought the tree, when, or how, did not really matter much to people of Father's generation. What mattered was that it was a *mulki* tree, a plant from the original homeland, and therefore special.

Tua Tua was one of the CSR's earliest sectors in Labasa, and one of the largest and the most prosperous, so people said, full of sturdy thatched homes, solid all-weather roads and rich red soil. Aja, my grandfather, completed his indenture there as a stable hand for the company's draught horses. When it ended in 1913, he moved to Tabia some five miles away. But since there was nothing in Tabia then, he continued to walk to Tua Tua to harvest cane and work as a general labourer on the CSR estates, keeping his connection alive to the place where it had all started for him, the first leg of his Fijian journey. The Tamarind Tree was his touchstone, his indispensable site of communion with his fellow girmitiyas living and dead alike.

I realise now, decades later, why the Tamarind Tree was so fondly remembered by the old-timers, what it meant to them. The Tree connected people to the past and served as a visible reminder of ancestral roots and routes. It was the initial point of entry for the new girmitiyas to the Tua Tua Sector. Five or ten years later, it would be the final point of departure for those whose girmit had ended, and who were now moving out to newer settlements opening up all around Labasa miles away from the sugar mill at the Qawa River. The Tree was the site of rest and respite from the relentless pace of plantation work. If the estate lines were decrepit and devoid of any sense of dignity and personal and social space, and full of the company's spies, the Tamarind Tree was a beacon of hope offering fleeting glimpses of freedom and opportunity on the other side of girmit. It was symbolically a source of renewal, rejuvenation and reassurance amidst all the confusions of dislocation and rupture. I have no doubt there were hundreds of tamarind, mango or banyan trees wherever girmitiyas were to be found, in Fiji and other sugar colonies around the world, which were witnesses to their special moments of triumphs and tragedies.

The departures provoked mixed emotion. Five years of working together in mills, in the cane fields, as domestic servants or as stable hands, and sharing the confined space in the lines, had bred a sense of companionship and camaraderie, a bond of friendship forged in circumstances of great adversity. That communal living, the security born of collective servitude, was coming to an end. No one knew where they might find land to settle or when they might meet again. They would now be on their own, starting all over again, often without a helping hand. Virgin land would have to be broken and brought into cultivation. Dangers lurked around every corner: flood, fire, wild pigs, theft of property, coercion by fellow men, violence. New relationships would have to be established, often with complete strangers and in unanticipated circumstances. New rules of social engagement would have to be developed, innovative ways found to minimise the inevitable frictions and conflicts in the newly emerging communities as people struggled to establish themselves and find a place they could call their own.

There were good reasons for apprehension, but many also felt a palpable sense of relief that girmit was only a temporary detention, not a life sentence as they had feared. For them, the end could not have come sooner. The newly freed were encouraged by stories of men who had farms of their own, grew their own crops, and built solid homes. Some were reported to have become big leaders, even moneylenders, in some settlements. With the arrival of families, children would be married off, schools started and ways found to give the nascent community a semblance of coherence and structure. In time, a new world would emerge, built with fragments from a remembered past but always, in the early days, haunted by the fear of the unknown, and the unthinkable prospect of failure. As people said, with Tolstoyan wisdom, everyone shared in your prosperity, but if you failed, you failed alone. The comfort of a settled, supportive community was yet some way into the future

It was under the Tamarind Tree that the newcomers were inducted into the culture and mores of the local estate, their home for the next five years or more. They would be told about the people to avoid, the overseers to be on the lookout for, the way to handle difficult tasks in the fields, and the tactics to employ to frustrate any unfair demands (tools could be damaged, sickness feigned, tasks completed slowly). They would learn where private pleasures in food and flesh could be safely indulged. For a little something on the side, anything was possible, anything could be arranged, cigarettes, alcohol, even women. Everyone knew who the best pimps and procurers in Tua Tua were. No wonder some girmitiyas called the estate lines *kasbighars* (brothels). If some plot had to be hatched about giving a hiding to a *sirdar* or an overseer, if some particularly troublesome girmitiya had to be put in his place or brought into line, if some company farm had to be torched in retaliation for violence against the labourers, the Tamarind Tree was the place to meet and plan. The plots hatched there and the secrets shared were safe.

Departures and arrivals, transactions and transitions: the Tamarind Tree was a silent witness to all these and much more. If only it could talk. From my scarce notes and fading memory, I recall imperfectly stories these men heard under the Tamarind Tree about the labyrinthine world of girmit. They are the partial, private recollections of old men, but they are all I have (perhaps all they had too). Like life itself, there is no single pattern to them, no single theme or narrative. Together, though, they provide an insight into a complex and conflicted world that is now well beyond recall. According to Ayesha Jalal, the noted Pakistan-born historian of the Indian subcontinent, 'It is possible to chalk out a new interdisciplinary way of reconnecting the histories of individuals, families, communities, and states in the throes of cataclysmic change.'[2] She goes on to suggest that 'Microhistorical detail can illuminate the texture of macrohistorical change.' The cause of historical scholarship would be enriched, Jalal argues, if investigations of historical causation were put on a collision course with the reality of individual lived experience. This essay could be viewed as just such a collision course.

As Father talked, his memories came flooding back in a way that completely surprised him, releasing a floodgate of long-forgotten emotions. They were as vivid and clear to him as broad daylight. He remembered accompanying Aja to the Wailevu market at the Tamarind Tree on Saturdays to sell the peanuts, maize, bean and

---

2   From the preface to her book *The Pity of Partition: Manto's Life, Times, and Work Across the India-Pakistan Divide* (New Jersey: Princeton University Press, 2013), p. xii. Her subject, Saadat Hasan Manto, wrote the incomparable short story, 'Toba Tek Singh'.

baigan he grew on his ten-acre farm. People from all around Wailevu came, men dressed in the traditional Indian garb of *dhoti* and *pagri* and long-flowing *kurta*. Buying and selling was really an excuse for weekly or monthly reunions. After five years of living together in the labour lines during the age of indenture, people had dispersed to wherever they could find a piece of land to rent. There was no rhyme or reason to how Indian settlements evolved. Contingency and circumstance determined outcomes. Meeting at the market under the Tamarind Tree kept the memories of old companionship alive. What Father remembered from those distant conversations was the clear consensus among the girmitiyas that fruits back home in India were always sweeter, the best. Indeed, everything about *mulk* (homeland) was golden, perfect: the nostalgia of a displaced people dealt a rough hand by fate. What strikes me now about the girmitiyas is how they were a people caught in-between, stranded in the cul-de-sac of a past vanishing before their eyes. They were living in a place they could not escape, making home in a land they could not fully embrace.

It was at gatherings under the Tamarind Tree that people recreated the rituals and ceremonies they remembered from their childhood back in India. Higher-caste men came to the market to have their weekly shave and regular haircut by their favourite *hajam*, traditional barbers, who would in return receive some lentils and rice. The ritual had to be observed even though everyone knew it to be just that, a ritual, Father said. It was their way of keeping a world alive even though they knew in their hearts that it was dead, for all practical purposes. Aja was no exception. Priests dispensed advice about the most propitious days for this *puja* (ritual) or that. Sometime in the 1920s, people built a small *kuti*, a small hut, near the Tamarind Tree, and priests took turns reading the scriptures and officiating at thanksgiving celebrations hosted by families in the hope of having a piece of good fortune or in anticipation of a blessing. This might be the birth of a son, for example, the cure of some mysterious ailment, or the lifting of a curse. Dates for festivals would be announced and taken to the settlements. Astrological charts would be drawn up for those who wanted it, names for babies suggested. People would make discreet enquiries about the availability of marriageable boys and girls. Marriages were still arranged by parents and community elders, preferably within a prescribed range of castes.

Caste rules were loosening and becoming unenforceable, but it was only a foolhardy man who would publicly breach community consensus about social mores and cultural practices. Father recalled the case of Hirwa who had unwittingly committed the heinous 'crime' of selling a cow to a Muslim. It was automatically assumed that the cow would be slaughtered for meat. For Hindus, the cow was mother incarnate. When the news became public, Hirwa was hauled before the elders, asked to do *prashchayat* (penance), and to give a *bhandara* (feast) for all his fellow village Hindus as well as a calf each to the three Brahmin families in the immediate neighbourhood. Breaching important social values could lead to *Huqqa-Pani-Bund*: social ostracism. People would be reluctant to marry into the family. They would avoid attending their funeral and mourning ceremonies. No *mandali* (group of disciples) would recite the *Ramayana* at their place. Cane fields might be torched, people beaten up, womenfolk interfered with. So a feast had to be given, whatever the cost. This could financially cripple the feast-giver, as happened with Hirwa. Broke and depressed, he left the village for some unknown place far away, leaving his past behind him. No one ever saw him again. The practice of punishing people using customary ways went with the old-timers, as the rule of tradition gradually gave way to the rule of law.

For Father, as a young boy, accompanying Aja to the annual festivals held at the Wailevu grounds was the most exciting time of the year. It was the same for children of my generation growing up without radio, television and other inventions now so commonplace. Ram Lila and Holi or Phagwa were the main festivals for the largely Hindu community around Wailevu. Ram Lila enacted the story of the *Ramayana*. For seven days the text would be read by groups of men, from different settlements taking turns, to the accompaniment of rudimentary musical instruments (*dholak*, harmonium, *dandtaal*). These could sometimes morph into intervillage competitions to see who 'sang' the *Ramayana* the best. The story of Rama, his childhood, exile and eventual triumphal return, would be acted out by men and boys with the right headgear and multicoloured clothes. People would sit rapt on the sack-covered ground witnessing the gripping drama being acted out before them by their own children or siblings. As a child, I relished playing the role of a monkey in Lord Hanuman's *baanar sena* (army) on its way to conquer Lanka, with my bouncy iron 'tail' wrapped in coloured crepe paper. Our performance would be the subject of much mirthful commentary at home and in school.

Phagwa was a more riotous affair, a festival of colours, celebrated at the end of the agricultural season on the last day of the lunar month. People played with coloured water and sprinkled powder on each other as they went from home to home singing *chautals* (specially composed songs). The climax came with the burning of the effigy of the evil king Hiranakashyap. A huge bonfire would light up the sky for all the neighbouring villages to see. One year, sparks from the bonfire set a nearby cane field alight, damaging several acres of the crop. That cause was disputed by some old-timers who thought people from another sector, jealous of the popularity of the Tamarind Tree celebrations, had torched the fields. Another theory had Muslims responsible because they resented the loud musical processions past the mosque especially during Friday prayers. Some blamed a family of thieves who were publicly shamed for stealing *murgi chor* (poultry). In typical village fashion, the speculations could be unending. Whatever the cause may have been, the CSR banned the celebrations at the Tamarind Tree for good. Thereafter, Phagwa became a local village-based celebration, and so it remains today.

Father's recollection of Phagwa reminded me of the Muslim festival of Mohurram (or Tazia) marking the martyrdom of Prophet Mohammed's grandsons, Hasan and Hussain. It was a public holiday in all the colonies which had taken advantage of Indian indentured labour. In the Caribbean, it was invariably associated with drunkenness. On that one day, people were allowed to let their hair down or, to change the metaphor, let off steam. Some latter day social theorists see the drunken behaviour 'as an act of resistance' against the planters, but it was probably little more than another excuse to have fun. Was there similar licence in Labasa? I asked Father. Alcohol was restricted to a few well-known and well-connected Indians, and the restrictions were not removed until the 1960s. But other drugs were around, principally *ganja* (marijuana, which old-timers from *biraadri*, comparable caste groups, smoked from a hookah in the *belo*, men's house). We children were not allowed near the building when the girmitiyas were talking about *aapas ke baat*: secret things. I still vividly remember the plants with serrated leaves at our well which we were told not to touch because they were 'holy.' Ganja gradually disappeared with the girmitiyas, though now it is making a comeback in some of the more remote parts of the country. *Yaqona*, or *kava*, became the principal social drink of the community, and alcohol when drinking restrictions were removed.

Kava, *Piper methysticum*, was the first Fijian item the Indians truly appropriated. It is a mildly narcotic drink, muddy in colour, made from the pounded root and stems of the plant. It was among the goods surreptitiously bartered with the Fijians who lived at the edge of the sugar estate. In exchange for salt, sugar, rice and spices, the Indians got fish, crab and prawns. These transactions were strictly illegal, for the government forbade contact between the two communities. The exchanges took place at the Tamarind Tree during late weekend afternoons or early evenings when chances of detection were slim. The old-timers remembered one Fijian man, Sekope, who was a regular at the Tamarind Tree: roly-poly, frequently shirtless, hairy-chested and a very savvy negotiator. '*Hum hiyan ke raja baitho*', he used to say, 'I am the king of this place.' He might have been, it is difficult to say. People remembered him as an open, friendly man but what they admired most was his fluency in the local variant of Hindustani, spiced with Fijian words and phrases and Hindi swear-words such as *sala chutia* (arsehole). The Tamarind Tree transactions crossed barriers and boundaries, but that was the extent of the interaction between the two communities. For the most part, the Fijians and the Indians continued to view each other through the prism of prejudice and fear.

The demanding plantation routine left the girmitiyas little time for idleness or indulgence. But weekends were free and during the drier months people gathered at the Wailevu grounds for fun and frivolity. *Gatka*, stick fighting, was popular but *kushti*, wrestling, was the main sport on the estates. It was familiar, cheap and entertaining and, more importantly, the CSR encouraged it as a way of keeping the men fit. Sometimes, it was staged as an inter-sector wrestling competition and sometimes as a contest between the free and those still under indenture. The prize did not matter, Father said, what counted was pride, in oneself and in one's sector. Rahiman, a recently freed labourer from Waiqele, was the champion wrestler widely known throughout Labasa. He was the man to beat. Once, a man named Jhagru challenged him to a contest. Everyone thought it would be a quick one-way contest, over in minutes if not seconds. But Jhagru had other ideas. He confided his plan to some close friends who decided to put a large sum of prize money behind him. Confident as ever, Rahiman's followers backed him with a similarly large sum, feeling almost sorry for his opponent. A large crowd gathered at the Tamarind Tree on the advertised day. As the two men were about to enter the 'ring', word spread that Jhagru had rubbed his body with pig fat. Rahiman, being a devout Muslim, refused even to shake hands with a pig-fat-smeared man, let alone wrestle with him and so forfeited the match, and the prize money. There was consternation in the crowd. Nothing like this had ever happened before, this act of pure provocation. Some applauded Jhagru's cunning audacity ('how did he ever think of *that!*') while others condemned his cowardly, potentially peace-disrupting act.

The hornet's nest had been disturbed. Rahiman's Muslim supporters, especially those who had backed him, were outraged at Jhagru's treachery and the insulting jeers and taunts of his supporters. Resentment had been building up among some Muslims who felt that Hindus were using their superior numbers to push them around. They were not being consulted on important decisions affecting everyone and were taken for granted. It was time to make a stand before they were reduced to nothing. The very next day, they slaughtered a calf in full view of some Hindu women washing clothes at the edge of the Wailevu River and began skinning the carcass which was strung from the branch of a mango tree. News of the slaughter spread like the proverbial wildfire in Wailevu and beyond. For Hindus, slaughtering cattle was bad enough, but doing it in such a brazen manner was provocative in the extreme. Frenzied meetings were held by both sides, and solemn oaths taken to teach a lesson that would not be forgotten for generations. Knives were sharpened and stones and sticks gathered for the inevitable bloody showdown. Someone even had a bucketful of pig's blood to throw down the wells of Muslims, for whom the pig is the filthiest of all animals and with which any form of contact is *haram*, forbidden. The whole community was on tenterhooks. Nothing less than their *izzat*, collective honour, was at stake and it had to be defended with blood, if it came to it. Lines in the sand could be drawn so easily and the gauntlet thrown down without a second thought.

Someone had the presence of mind to report the matter to the Tua Tua Sector Office. Mr Sebastian immediately drove to the Tamarind Tree and gathered leaders of both communities for an urgent meeting. Mr Sebastian was trusted as few other overseers were. Unable to pronounce his name, people had dubbed him Mr Subhas Chand. He had been at Tua Tua for several years. 'This is CSR land', he told the leaders, and no disturbance would be tolerated on it. 'What will the other sectors think? Have you thought of the reputation of this place, your reputations? Do you want to go to gaol for something stupid such as this?' '*Badmashi bund*', he declared, stop this nonsense. 'No more Kushti from now on. Kushti *khatam*', he said with an air of finality as he got up to leave. '*Tum sab ghare jao aur chuppe baitho*' (now you all go home and do not disturb the peace). '*Ji Saheb*' (yes, sir), people said, feeling suitably chastised. Everyone breathed a sigh of relief that a certain bloody confrontation had been avoided. The leaders regretted the foolishness of their reckless hot-headedness and agreed not to allow things to develop to this stage in future.

A resolution of sorts was reached a week or so later when at a gathering of both communities under the Tamarind Tree, Jhagru apologised to Rahiman and shared half the prize money with him. Soon afterwards, for reasons then unknown, he left Wailevu for Wainikoro in northern Vanua Levu. People later said that this was Mr Sebastian's handiwork. As an experienced overseer and observer of the Indians, he realised that the truce was temporary, like a patch over the puncture of an overheating tyre. Sooner or later, it would erupt. Grief and grievance ran deep among the people Mr Sebastian had long supervised. It was one trait the company and colonial officials knew and feared: the unpredictable reaction of a people who on the surface appeared so docile. If Jhagru left Tua Tua voluntarily, Mr Sebastian reportedly said, there would be no black mark against his name. Nor against his own for letting matters get out of hand in a place which he knew like the back of his palm. Jhagru agreed; he really had little choice. A few months later, Mr Sebastian was promoted and transferred to another estate.

Father was not alone in his almost mystical reverence for the Tamarind Tree. His recollections led me to other older men in the village – Nikka, Bihari, Mallu, Genda, Digambar – who had their own stories to tell about the Tree. They, too, recalled the festivals, the food and the fun they had as children, making their weekly pilgrimages to the Wailevu market with their fathers. Nikka remembered Madho, an Ahir cow herd, who was very particular about caste scruples and practices. The Ahirs had a reputation as tough and independent-minded peasants, never shirking a fight in defence of personal or family honour or when avenging a real or imagined insult. Girmit had turned Madho's world upside down. The basic tenets of the old order of village India were gone or had become irrelevant, but he was determined to preserve what he could of the old ways. He would work with men of all castes; in this he had no choice, but he cooked his own meals whenever he could. He would take food and drink only from men of his own caste or those above him. And he managed to create a small fraternity of Ahirs in Tua Tua, a *biradari*. Its main purpose was to maintain a semblance of Ahir cultural identity. They performed remembered rituals for their *kul devtas* (family gods and goddesses), celebrated their ancient village festivals, helped each other whenever they could, and performed the *Ahirwa ke naatch*[3] at festive occasions and weddings. We in Tabia knew it as *Lehnga ke naatch*. Now it is gone, replaced by mindless Bollywood extravaganzas and Michael Jackson-style dancing.

---

3   A special Ahir dance performed by a man dressed in women's clothes.

The most important role of the *biradari* was to arrange marriage for Ahir children. Madho invariably took the lead in the negotiations. Marrying 'down' was out and so was marrying up into castes much higher than your own. It was *adharmic*, morally inappropriate, potentially inviting divine retribution. These caste arrangements were the work of the gods, not of men, Madho used to say. Old-timers, Nikka said, kept a careful mental record of where eligible boys and girls were. Some even arranged marriages as soon as children were born. This was the practice among some castes in village India. Once given, one's word was cast in stone. Sometimes, things could go too far. Once Madho had a man caned under the Tamarind Tree in front of his fellow Ahirs for eloping with a woman of lower caste (Chamar). Caste pollution, he had said, set a bad example. When the senior sector manager, Mr Harriman, (Hari Ram to the girmitiyas) came to know of the incident, he told Madho, whom he otherwise respected for his leadership abilities, not to take matters into his own hands. *'Hiyan hum sarkar baitho'*, he said (here we are the government). Madho remained Madho to the end, incorrigible and unreformed, but with progressively diminishing authority and influence, a relic of a forgotten past, as people dispersed and new influences came. In time, wealth and education, not caste, became the markers of identity and status.

Labasa sugar plantations had a reputation for inflicting excessive violence on girmitiyas. Files record men and women travelling long distances, from Nagigi and Wainikoro and Laga Laga, under cover of darkness to report cases of abuse to the stipendiary magistrate in Nasea town, taking so much risk of discovery but with no guarantee of redress. Indian sirdars (foremen), oral tradition had it, were the lynchpins of the system, who played pimps and procurers for their masters. In return, they received small favours allowing them to make extra money on the side, such as running the estate store or doing minor moneylending. It was not all one-way traffic though, as I learned. Sirdars and everyone else well knew the dangers as well, the limits beyond which it was not prudent to venture. The sharpened cane-knife in the hands of an enraged man was the most feared weapon on the plantation, with killers freely confessing their crimes before facing the gallows. This kind of violence was not uncommon in village India: *'izzat ke sawal hai'*, people said, it is a question of honour. Honour, their sense of self respect, was all they had. It was the way of the peasant world.

Bhukkan was the go-to man should one want to teach someone a lesson. He liked to see himself as the peoples' enforcer in the sector. Members of his caste had taken that *dhandha* (role), even in India, it was said. Perhaps he was from one of those 'criminal tribes' Europeans had written so much about. Bhukkan looked the part too, people said: dark, tall, broad-chested, with a face full of week-long growth and stylishly twirled moustache. He would take care of the offender for a little something. The attack had to be carefully planned over weeks to avoid detection, especially as the lines were full of CSR eyes and ears. And it had to be proportionate to the offence given or crime committed. An unwritten code of conduct was observed, even on remote Fijian plantations, perhaps a remnant of village India. Bhukkan had four or five henchmen who were like blood brothers to him. They would meet under the Tamarind Tree at night in complete secrecy. The nature of the offence would be ascertained and the appropriate punishment determined. Then, over the next few weeks, the movements of the offending man would be closely but unobtrusively monitored: the route he took to work, the time he returned to the barracks, who his close friends were. *Khabardari*, alertness, was the name of the game.

The man giving offence this time was Sukkha, the sirdar who liked to make a 'cheek-pass' at the women who worked under him. He had an eye for Janakia, Jaggan's wife, making sexually suggestive remarks within her hearing, casually letting his hand roam over his crotch while giving her orders for the day's fieldwork. Jaggan himself was helpless to do anything. If he remonstrated, he would be isolated from the rest of his coworkers, given a heavier task and perhaps even whipped. He had seen that happen too many times to too many men to take the risk. He knew that no one would come to his assistance, as they all feared Sukkha's whip-hand and, even more, the overseer's boots. Overseer-sirdar collusion was common enough on the plantations, and it was the deadliest of all the possible permutations and combinations of men. Jaggan pleaded with Bhukkan to save his *izzat*. 'I have no one here. You are my *mai-baap*, *Dada*', he said, my benefactor, sir. He would do anything for him in return, even sacrifice his life for him. Bhukkan agreed to take a bottle of rum and two fat roosters for this relatively easy assignment, and a plan of attack began to be hatched at the Tamarind Tree over several nights.

On the designated day, Bhukkan and his men agreed to go to the remotest part of the estate to clean out the overgrown drains in preparation for the rainy season. Sukkha came to inspect the work at the end of the day as the sun was about to go down. It was then the men set upon him, dragging him deep into the cane field where no one could see or hear them. They pinned him to the rough ground and took turns urinating in his mouth and all over his body, using the choicest swear words they could think of. '*Sala maadharchod* (motherfucker), you are doing this to your own mothers and sisters? *Haramil* (bastard), what kind of *Jaanwar* (animal) are you? *Bhonsriwala* (son of a whore). *Mutimilelie* (may you be mixed with earth). Next time, we will shove this *lathi* (heavy iron-bound stick) up your arse', they said menacingly. 'And then we will take good care of your wife while you watch.' For good measure, they stripped him of his pants and ordered him back to the barracks pantless. The humiliation was as complete as it was brutal. The next day, Sukkha asked to be transferred to another estate. No one ever saw him in Tua Tua again.

From sirdars the talk moved seamlessly to sahibs, the overseers whom the girmitiyas called Kulambars, reportedly coined from the order they barked, 'Call your number.' Names were often recalled in formal form: Mr Jones, Mr Taylor, Mr Davidson, the Burra Sahibs and the Chota Sahibs, the head and the junior overseers. Some were known only by their nicknames, such as Tamaatar (an overseer whose face was perennially red in the bright sun), Ullu who seemed clueless most of the time, and Luccha who had crude habits (farting loudly in public) and a penchant for using mispronounced Hindi swear words, especially about female genitalia. The overseers came in all shapes and sizes, people said, never fitting a single stereotype. If you did your work and completed your task, they left you alone, people said, but if you tried to be a smart-arse, they would quickly find out and give you the hiding of your life, and you would become a marked man. Then you were fair game; your fate was sealed.

Some overseers got very attached to the place where they worked and the people they supervised. Some would come to the Tamarind Tree, usually on a Sunday, to tell the people that they were being transferred to another sector and ask them to be as good with their successors as they had been with them. Sometimes those who had served in the sector for a long time would bring along a few loaves of bread and cans of jam, or donate a goat as parting gift, and people would give them homemade sweets, such as *satua* or *lakdi ke mithai,* a particular favourite. Nothing was said, no promises made or extracted but much was understood by both sides. Such strategic exchanges, some anthropologists might say, had powerful symbolic meanings and internal logic of their own, deployed at critical points to achieve desired outcomes. Probably. The girmitiyas might have been simple people but they were certainly not simpletons.

Mr Underwood was not one of those *sharif* (honourable) overseers. He was a strange type, Digambar recalled, a man of few words but free and furious with whips and fist, punching and kicking people whenever the mood seized him, screaming at the top of his screechy voice so that others heard him clearly. But that was not the worst thing about him as there were many others around Labasa whose reputation for violence was just as bad. Underwood's real problem was that he had a taste for men. He would paw his prey in some isolated corner of the plantation and bugger them, certain that his victims would never publicly confess the assault for fear of shame. With time, Underwood got bolder and more brazen, and word of his bizarre behaviour spread beyond Tua Tua.

Something had to be done. Even people from other sectors were beginning to make enquiries, never a good sign. No one had much respect for a man who had been buggered, a *gandu*, who could not defend his own honour. There was nothing more shaming than being called a sector of effeminate *gandus*. Bhukkan was approached. He convened a meeting under the Tamarind Tree at which several people admitted sexual assault, including Mangal, whom Bhukkan regarded as a younger brother. They were *jahajibhais* (ship mates) from the *Sangola*. The assaults ascertained, the question was what the punishment should be? Bhukkan had no doubt that it had to be death, and a violent one at that. A lesson had to be taught that *mardaanagi* (Indian manhood) was not to be trifled with.

On the designated day, Bhukkan and his men lay in wait as Underwood made his way on horseback to his favourite spot on the estate behind the mango tree. He fell to the ground when a huge stone hit him on the back of the head. The men dragged him to the middle of the cane field and in a murderous rage hacked him to pieces. They then stuffed dismembered parts of his body into a jute sack, tied it up and buried it in a grave in the overgrown grass at the far end of the field, covering it with shrubs to avoid detection. The gruesome murder shook the CSR. Underwood's depravity was known to his fellow overseers and he would have been transferred to another sector sooner or later, or assigned a non-supervisory position in the company's local office. That would be the common practice for dealing with the 'rotten potatoes', as the phrase went, before the whole sack was lost.

But the labourers had to be taught a lesson lest things got out of hand and the company's authority in the public eye was undermined. Strong resolve was called for, and the company left no stone unturned in getting to the bottom of the matter, with the support of the local inspector of police. The area's stipendiary magistrate, Mr Foster, a former CSR overseer, agreed and urged swift action. Workers had to be put firmly in their place. For weeks, people were beaten or bribed for leads. Wages were withheld and permission refused for labourers to leave the estate, even for brief social visits. Nor were visitors allowed to enter the estate premises. The estate dispensary was allowed to run out of medicine. All recreational activities were cancelled. The Tua Tua estate was in complete lockdown mode. Many suspected who the deed-doer was but no one said anything. Treachery and betrayal at a time like this would bring swift retribution, usually in the form of beheading. And Underwood was a bad man. Then someone – Chotu, people found out much later, with whose wife Bhukkan was having a torrid affair – fingered Bhukkan as the most likely culprit. He admitted leading the assault as an act of self defence against egregious provocation. 'First our women, then our men; who is next, our children?', he reportedly said at the trial, but to no avail. He was found guilty of first-degree murder and hanged and his co-conspirators sentenced for life.

The plantation was clearly a place of rough, rudimentary justice. The girmitiyas often did not get a fair day in the courts. The mysterious protocols of *Court-Kachehri* (the courts) were beyond them, and cases were decided on the basis of hard evidence adduced, not on hearsay or uncorroborated assertion. Inevitably, the overseers came out on top. But the stories I heard suggested greater complexity. Excesses certainly occurred but they came at a price, everyone realised, and usually at the expense of life. Things could go only so far and no further. Tact was backed by force. It was people like the men who gathered under the Tamarind Tree who maintained a semblance of order at a time of great chaos and confusion and kept the community intact. It was no mean achievement to transform a rag-tag group of people from hundreds of castes, speaking a host of tongues, from different parts of the subcontinent, subjected to servitude on the plantations, into a relatively smoothly functioning community bound by some essential values. It was not until much later that I realised why the old-timers held the names of men like Bhukkan in such awe and admired them so much. They were their unsung heroes, *samaj rakshak*, guardians of the community.

On a fleeting visit to Labasa some years ago, I went to the site of the Tamarind Tree late one afternoon. Nothing remained but the rotten stump of the old Tree concealed in the tall, unruly grass. School children walked past the site every day, unaware of what once was there. Not even the teachers at Wailevu Primary knew. It was the same with the men cutting cane in adjacent fields and others going about their daily business on horseback or bicycles. The silence was surreal, almost haunting. The past had become past, just like that. It reminded me of so many other things I had seen or experienced but which were now gone. I remembered the graves I had seen some years earlier of men and women who had died during the wreck of the *Syria*, now lying unmarked and covered by shrubs at the edge of the Nasilai village. I remembered the tall mango tree behind our thatched house in Tabia which had given us the fruit for our pickles, but which had been destroyed after a fire, lit to smoke the bees out from its hollowed base, had been left to smoulder away for months. The land where we had grown up, where so many of our childhood memories were formed, has been reclaimed by its native owners and has reverted to bush, obliterating all signs of the life and laughter that once filled the place. Signs of dereliction and neglect abound. That is typical of so many Indian settlements throughout Vanua Levu. There is little consciousness of the past and even less desire to know about it among our people. Everyone is trying to leave, hoping eventually to migrate overseas. My own links to Labasa have become tenuous over the years as members of our extended family have left the island to settle in other parts of Fiji. Tabia, the village where I grew up, is now a place of evanescent memories. All the old markers of special moments have disappeared.

Father died nearly twenty years ago. We did not really know him when he was alive; we hardly ever talked about private matters. That was the way things were then. I understand the reason for his grief better now than I did before: the death of the world that formed him. I think I understand the man better, too, his fears and hopes and his sense of his place and purpose on earth. I understand all that, but I also understand why the Tamarind Tree went, why it had to go. It had come to Tua Tua with the girmitiyas and now, ever so faithfully, it was going out with them, taking with it their secrets and the stories of their hopes and aspirations. The Tree had given succour and security to men and women from the old world but it had little meaning or relevance to those who followed them. Its long journey had finally come to an end in May 1962 when it was hit by lightning and razed. *Finis coronat opus.* A reminder of another time and place, its demise lay to rest the ghosts of the past: people like Bhukkan and Underwood and countless others. Befittingly, like so many girmitiyas, it died, with its dignity intact, a sudden, uncomplicated death, not a long, lingering one. The Tamarind Tree was gone but not forgotten: its ashes would continue to nourish the soil, soil of Father's generation and mine.

'I go sen' for you'

Fawzia Muradali Kane

Rasheedan　　　　　　　　　　　　　　　　　　*Boodhanie*

My family refused him, said his skin
was too dark. He built them a palace.

> My husband once saw a mongoose battle
> a snake while cane stalks were being set alight.

One night he came to my window.
I wrapped jasmine sheets with dowry gold.

> He led the way for me through the fields.
> The mongoose bit the snake, then smoke covered them.

I walked with him along two hundred miles
of railway tracks, from the mountains to the sea.

> I raised my cutlass each half year, bent my back
> to plant ratoons, before the dry season ended.

The child in my belly bucked more
than the ship that sailed over black water.

> My arms grew strong, my skin turned
> a midnight sheen. My hair thinned to white.

My son was born four days after my feet touched
the stone outcrop of that island.

He collected my 16 cents a day wage, held on to his 25,
said he saved it for us to go back over the water.

My husband could read, they made him a driver of gangs.
I never worked in the fields, the sun hurt my eyes.

When our ten years were done, he put the coins
in a brass pot, wrapped it in a cotton dhoti.

My skin stayed smooth. My sons carried books
to school, their sons taught the sons of others.

He sailed back home with all we possessed, alone.
Each night, I would tell my daughters of his promise.

My youngest brother had followed, refused to sign
any bond, paid his way to look for me.

He would build us a palace, with a garden of
pomegranate trees, and a fountain scented with jasmine.

Ten years later my brother found me, I held him while he cried,
curled in my lap like the baby I remembered.

Each half-year season, I waited for the rain to break
the noonday heat. Every morning, I sharpened my blade.

*My great-great-grandmothers arrived in Trinidad c.1860. One had left her
wealthy family in Uttar Pradesh to elope with a married man. The other
was abandoned at the end of the contract, left to bring up her three young
daughters alone.*

Paradise Island

Priya N. Hein

It was a beautiful wintry evening when the children arrived at
Grand Dada[1] and Grand Dadi's[2] Creole-style house facing the
sea. The gentle murmur of the waves lapping against the white
sand was occasionally interrupted by the sounds of distant motor-
boats coming back from a day's fishing. There was a visitor on the
porch, sitting comfortably in the wicker chair, sipping the strong
homemade cinnamon-flavoured rum Grand Dada had offered him.

'Tell us a story, Grand Dada. Please!', begged the children. Grand
Dada shook his head. 'No, children. You'll have to wait a little while,
until I finish cleaning the fresh fish Gaston just brought us. Grand Dadi
is making her special fish biryani tomorrow', he said with a chuckle.

The children eyed the scruffily dressed fisherman curiously.
He smiled shyly at them as he savoured Grand Dada's spicy rum.
'Oh, I'll tell you a story if you want', he suggested, not wishing to
disappoint the children. Grand Dada nodded at him as he scratched
off the transparent fish scales with a sharp knife, sending them flying
all around him. Gaston downed the rest of his drink and squinted
his eyes, as if recollecting a distant memory. The children waited
patiently, not wanting to disturb his train of thought. Suddenly,
Gaston opened his eyes, stared into the distance, at the sea, and
began his story...

*

'There was once a magnificent constellation of islands in the Indian
Ocean that was like paradise', he began in a calm, soothing voice. 'The
sea was the most exquisite shade of crystal-clear turquoise, inhabited
by turtles and a wide variety of colourful tropical fish, surrounded
by unspoiled coral reefs. The children often played alongside the
tortoises and the giant crabs on the beautiful beaches, underneath
the shade of the coconut trees which grew abundantly. They could
be heard laughing and playing on the beach till late at night under
the magnificent starry sky which sparkled like diamonds.

1   In Indian families, dada is the paternal grandfather.
2   Dadi is the paternal grandmother.

The inhabitants were the descendants of African slaves and Indian labourers who had settled on the islands in the eighteenth century to work on the vast coconut plantations. Although poor, they lived contentedly. They led quiet but happy lives.

There was a boy nicknamed Takamaka because of all the time he spent under the shade of the big takamaka tree not far from his bungalow. Takamaka was a happy boy and, just like the other boys of the island, he liked to go out to sea on his pirogue to fish. Once back on shore, the children would share their catch. When the sun began to set and the last light of the sun shimmered on the ocean, families would gather in front of their small cement houses to fry the freshly-caught fish in an old blackened pan with a little coconut oil, garlic and fresh chillies from the garden.

They would eat the fish, still sizzling hot, with their hands, followed by *mouf*, a mixture of ground rice, sugar and coconut milk wrapped in fresh banana leaves gently cooked in boiling water until it reached a soft texture, which melted in the mouth. The subtle taste of the rice cooked in fresh coconut milk from the plantations was simply divine.

One day, Takamaka's younger sister Sibil, aged six, fell ill. Mami and Papi were concerned about her deteriorating health and decided to take her to the mainland to see a doctor. As a talisman, Takamaka made Sibil a small necklace out of a piece of coconut string passed through a hole he had pierced in a *coquille bonheur*[3] shell. It was a particularly shiny shell which had caught the sun's rays and sparkled at Takamaka as he swam underwater, not far from the reef. Its pearly colour seemed to have been painted on using several layers of thick gloss.

'Here's a little present for you. It'll bring you luck', said Takamaka as he reassured his little sister that everything would be fine. Takamaka promised Sibil that he would make her a matching armband when she returned to the island. As Sibil was too weak to respond, she merely smiled at Takamaka, and he gently tied the chain around her dainty neck. Papi asked Takamaka to look after his Mami and two other sisters while he was away.

The next day, Papi and Sibil set off for Mauritius. Takamaka and the rest of the family watched sadly as Papi carried Sibil away in his arms, given that she was too feeble to walk up the ramp leading to

---

3   Cowrie shell.

the ship. Their figures seemed tiny in contrast to the great cargo ship that was to cross the Indian Ocean.

Back on the island, the rest of the family was waiting impatiently for their return, praying that Sibil would be cured of her illness and be back home in no time. However, the days turned into weeks and the weeks into months and they were still not back from the mainland. In the meantime, strange things were happening on their once peaceful island.

There were now white men in strange uniforms taking pictures and notes and talking in a foreign tongue. The children felt intimidated. They no longer played on the beach as freely, and the adults were whispering to each other, worried about various rumours floating around the island. 'Things are going to change', they said. They could feel it.

There was a bad energy circling the island. Even the fish were becoming scarce, scared of the dark energy looming around, as if they too were aware of a lurking premonition.

One day, Takamaka went into the woods to gather sticks for Mami to make a fire. Takamaka heard a muffled sob coming from behind a banyan tree. As he gingerly approached the tree, he discovered a boy squatting in the shade, hugging his knees. He looked miserable, thought Takamaka, as if he were carrying a huge weight on his frail shoulders. 'What's the matter?', asked Takamaka. The boy looked up in surprise. At first, he did not answer and quickly looked away. He eventually looked up again and told Takamaka that his dog had disappeared just like the others.

Takamaka hurried home and asked what was happening on the island, why the dogs were disappearing. Mami held him tight and told him they would have to leave their island. 'But why?', asked Takamaka, who failed to understand why he had to leave his home. Mami shrugged her skinny shoulders and sighed in response. 'I wish I knew' she almost whispered to herself.

As the boats that delivered rations to the islands stopped visiting, the neighbours, once very friendly, started bickering with each other over nothing. They no longer wanted to share their fruits and vegetables, afraid that food was becoming incredibly scarce.

A few days later, Takamaka had a nightmare. He was sitting alone on the beach, staring at the sea, when suddenly he saw another larger island opposite him. In the distance, he could see his younger sister Sibil wearing a pristine white cotton dress. She was slowly walking towards the sea as if in a trance. As she stepped into the clear lagoon, the water around her suddenly turned muddy, a stark contrast to the clear turquoise it used to be. Behind Sibil were tall white men wearing military uniforms, running after her. All of a sudden, dogs began to howl.

The howling got louder and louder until Takamaka woke up in the middle of the night covered in sweat. As he turned around, he noticed that Mami was up too. She was looking out of their small window in fear. When he realised that the howling was actually coming from outside, he asked Mami what was going on. 'They are gassing the dogs', she whispered in the dark. 'It's a warning. First they cut our food supplies, and now they exterminate our dogs. We will have to leave the island very soon.'

The next morning, every single dog had disappeared from the island. The inhabitants were informed that they had to evacuate their home within the hour. They were allowed one piece of luggage per family. As most families did not possess a suitcase, they had to wrap all their belongings in a bed sheet or an old pillowcase.

Takamaka carefully wrapped the pretty armband he had made for Sibil in a banana leaf. 'At least we'll see Papi and Sibil again', said Mami as she packed their meagre possessions into their one and only battered suitcase. From the deck of the ship, Takamaka held Mami's hand and they watched their island grow smaller and smaller, both wondering when and if they would ever see it again.

It was a ghastly journey. No one said much as they were in shock, still bewildered. After a few days of travelling, which felt like forever, they were finally offloaded in Mauritius and taken to new homes that looked like abandoned barracks. Trapped in a prison, that's how they felt. The small, dimly-lit rooms had no windows and were infested with rats and cockroaches. Gone were the days of freedom when Takamaka and his friends could play without a care on the beach. He failed to understand why they were being punished. Nothing reassured his father, whom he could hardly recognise. Papi had become bony, his face so hollow it was almost scary to look at its protruding eyes. Although it had been only a few months since Takamaka had last seen Papi, he looked at least a decade older. His eyes were underlined with dark circles and contained a profound sadness that Takamaka had never seen before.

When Sibil died, Papi was told he could not return to his island because it had been sold by the British government to the Americans to make way for a military base. Most of the inhabitants of the islands, known as the Chagos Archipelago, never saw their home again. Many died on the horrible journey to Mauritius or in exile, never getting over the pain of being forced to leave their island.'

*

'Did Takamaka ever get to see his island again?', asked one of the children.

'No', replied Gaston, shaking his head sadly. He stayed silent for a while staring at the sea.

He then added, 'Who knows? Maybe one day, the Chagos Islands will become theirs again.'

As he got up to leave, something fell out of his pocket. One of the children, sitting near his wicker chair, picked it up. It was a child's armband on which was tied the most exquisite *coquille bonheur* shell.

Building Walls

Kama La Mackerel

in 1986, two decades into post-independent Mauritius

on an island where the carcasses of power
have just been transferred to a broken people
where a population feeds on opportunism
like dregs of banana wine in the hollow of a bottle

on an island where insecurity trembles like magma in the veins between
        kréol   laskar   malbar madras
           ti-nation   gran-nation
where the smell of trauma hangs like dried octopus under the sun

my parents each hold a kid in one arm and from their free hand

                                                    they sign

grandchildren of girmitiyas – 'the agreement people'
inheritors of a corrupt british understanding of a contract
birthed from thumbprints on a faithless document
like passports in a language they did not even understand

my parents sign on a piece of paper

my parents sign

        their first mortgage.

        the first mortgage in family history.
        land-owning mortgage.
        french speaking mortgage.
        government job mortgage.
        colour-tv-mortgage.
        maybe-even-a-car-someday mortgage.

114

on the island of emancipation where power is up for grabs
dreams are clouded with ancestral hopes:
artifacts made of gold can be found

under rocks

if you dig

long and hard enough

or if you know the right uncle's neighbour
or if your cousin is married to a minister's daughter
or if you serve whiskey, lamb biryani and rasgullas in a thick envelope to
the fat-bellied man in a white shirt

the island is parched like dried mud on a sand bank
thirsting for poetic justice that reeks like rust
ti-dimoune, grand-dimoune – ca kenn tente zot sanse

in 1986 my parents absolve themselves from plantation heritage
signing themselves into a lifetime of repayment

they buy a piece of land on which leans

a room

an outdoors toilet

an outdoors kitchen

formerly the residence of servants and domestics on the edge of white
people property

they fill the space with a bed, two mattresses, a cupboard, two boxes of
tableware, an iron, a sewing machine
enough faith and commitment to keep our four bodies warm as we sleep
under a roof we still don't dare call ours

over the next twenty years this roof will stretch   itself   over   our heads
like new constellations being written to bear witness to the whispers of my
parents
as they brainstorm budget scheme plot plan dream late into the night

by 1990, we have a living room and an extra bedroom that my brother and
i share
by 1992, we have an indoors kitchen and an indoors toilet
by 1996, on the cusp of entering adolescence, i finally inherit my own
bedroom

by the turn of the millennium, we have a separate prayer room where we
burn incense sticks to honour our many gods, goddesses, saints, visionaries
and prophets

by 2004, all the ground surfaces of the house are carefully tiled and my
father spends three months conceiving a mosaic on the terrace floor with
the left-over tiles

by 2006, my parents are done building their house. our house.

it took them twenty years

twenty years of stacks of bricks and piles of rock-sand we considered our
kin

twenty years of layers of dust sprayed like a grey film on our skin

twenty years when i watched my father make miracles with his bare hands
and arched back

like a super-hero he parted the ground underneath our feet to lay the
foundation of our safety

like a wizard he rose walls from dead earth to offer shelter to our bodies

       surfaces of security   walls of redemption

                 the alchemy of mixed concrete

   the anagram of placed bricks   that he carefully arranged

                 like scrabble tiles

      over this piece of land   he wanted to claim as ours

every space in this house, our house, my house
(the house i left behind, ran away from)
speaks of my father

the surfaces smell of his cemented hat soaked in sweat
the roof heats up like the burnt skin of his cheeks
the tiled floors slip like his glass-frames off his nose
the walls have the callused texture of his dried hands like sandpaper
every door frames his pout   his lower lip pushed forward
every window reflects the assiduity of his gaze
the empty depth in the black of his eyes

for twenty years i watched my father build this house
trampling his hands like bagasse
burning his bones like arak

creating his life's work in the language of men
who were forced to cut their tongues and hang them
like cautionary tales on sugar-cane stalks
their silence a stout echo like sea foam haunting   the   island   from
                                                     shore   to   shore

for twenty years i watched the walls come up around us

as the house grew

so did the silence of my father

the walls echoed his absence   his voice never to be heard   his
dissociation a stillness reflected   in the sulkiness of his work   in
the sipping of his afternoon tea   in the sting of his right-hand against
my child's face when he caught me in a dress   in how he leaves the
radio on so he doesn't have to hear our voices   in how he reads all
the time so he doesn't have to engage with us – pamphlets, flyers, sunday
newspapers sprawled like left-over food over the dinner table   the first
time he visited me in canada   he read the box of salt over lunch during
our first meal together

my father lived up to his inheritance
the oldest son in a house with nine kids

i wonder whether he dreams in silence at night
extracting his vocal cords like a fishnet full of water

whether he has visions of his grandmother
crouched in a hold with the burn of iron under her breast

whether he sees the face of his mother
the day she died
                    of an abortion
after she'd already given birth
                                        nine times

for twenty years i watched my father's mechanical body wear itself out
as the years went by, he seemed to get smaller and smaller
i never really quite knew whether it was him getting smaller
or the walls around us getting higher

my father built built built built built
more rooms, a garage, a verandah, a backyard
spaces that he filled with his silence
an absent presence, a present absence
ghostly like silky butterflies with torn wings

as the surfaces spread around us
so did the distance between our bodies
so did the distance between the words we exchanged

so did the expanses of the walls
within which my father trapped his feelings

so did the thickness of the paint
with which he shielded his heart

my father lived up to the legacy of men
who were taught to swallow their tongues
scythe languages of love

this house though speaks
this house speaks of him
in an invisible language
only men like him know how to use
the legacy of torn muscles, cracked bones, hands at work
never stopping

in this house is trapped his life's work

his silence

his silence

in his silence   i hear the ghosts of our ancestors   our long lineage
            of displaced   misplaced people
        cramped into   the house he built   the promised legacy
            not a tomb   not a monument
just a place   they can   we can   finally call home.

The Legend of Nagakanna

Aneeta Sundararaj

(from *The Age of Smiling Secrets*, a novel)

Nandini stood inside the marquee and looked around at the business of everything. Her mother, Kamini, had her back to her. Nandini shook her head. What was she talking about? No such thing as a birthday party. These open days, held on the same day every year, were an excuse to make money.

Within a few years of the family business, Jasmine Crochets, operating as a private limited company, Kamini had built a substantial list of clients, customers and suppliers. To celebrate their success, Kamini hosted an annual open day on 8 August. In the days before the celebrations, the Sungai Petani house teemed with people. Caterers prepared delicious food and a marquee was set up in the garden in case it rained. At any given time, there were more than twenty women crocheting hundreds of items for sale. All these items were sold during the open day. By about 5 pm, a group of invited guests would gather around Kamini to receive samples of items still in the early stages of production in Jasmine Crochets. If their response was favourable, these prototypes would become part of next year's collection. There was also an auction for a one-off creation by Jasmine Crochets, the proceeds of which would be divided among the workers to help fund their children's education. Then came an intimate party to celebrate Nandini's birthday.

Nandini glanced at Kamini's latest creation – a bedspread with a picture of a house by the side of a kidney-shaped stream. There was a mango-coloured ribbon pulled through the loops at the border for definition. This looked familiar. A smile of recognition. She learned to swim here. Nandini looked up. Her mother's back was still to her. This was her chance.

For the first time in seven years, Nandini crossed the drain at the back of the Sungai Petani house and ventured deep into Foothills Estate. The further along she walked, the thicker the ground cover became. Unseen by the sun, the moss-covered roots of the rubber trees bulged. The living pillars, black and rough, extended high above the ground before they disappeared into a natural canopy of dark green leaves.

Nandini came to a clearing. When she turned a corner, she saw a bridge. Across it, there was a motorbike outside the front door of a dwelling place. She recognised the red helmet on the seat. Karuppan's helmet.

What was he doing here?

'Karuppan?'

Karuppan stood by the window and looked out.

Kamini's child. Kamini's walk. Kamini's eyes. But the child's hair was wild. This was insane. If he turned down the volume of the television, she would know he was avoiding her. If he allowed her inside, then...

What if she was like her father? The kind of person who called people like Karuppan that filthy name – estate boy.

Karuppan opened the front door. 'Nandini', he called out.

Nandini looked up. Karuppan was standing with his legs apart and hands placed firmly on his hips. He was a tall man, at least six inches taller than her mother. Imposing. Authoritative. She smiled and crossed the bridge. 'What are you doing here?' she asked.

'What about you, Kanna?' He used her nickname on purpose. 'Shouldn't you be at your birthday party?'

'Huh! The party is not for me.'

Karuppan gave a broad smile and the muscles on his face relaxed. He invited her inside and she surveyed the place: the television with an internal antenna, his sofa, kitchen, two pots, one pan, two plates and a stove. At the threshold of his bedroom, she turned to face him. 'Sorry. Nosey.' Her one-sided smile showed her embarrassment.

'No problem', he said. 'Sit down.' He waved his hand towards the dining table.

'Thank you. This place is beautiful.'

'Thank you.'

'You live here alone?', she asked, sitting down at the small dining table.

'Yes', he answered, focusing on a spot on the wall above Nandini's head. When he returned from Kuala Lumpur five years ago, his enquiries at the Land Registry Office revealed that no one owned this place that he'd once named 'Kamini's Winter Palace'. He decided then to make it his. Metal beams were inserted in key places to fortify the structure. Slabs of asbestos and red tiles replaced the *attap*[1] roof. Rainwater that collected in gutters was channelled into a pipe that led to the stream behind the house. The beams on the white walls were painted black – an English cottage in the heart of a tropical rubber estate.

Karuppan never spoke of this place. He let others assume that he was in the city whenever he wasn't in town. In fact, he'd spend many nights in this, his sanctuary. But it never occurred to him that there was an unseen being watching his every move.

'So, what brings you here?'

'Nothing', Nandini shrugged. She twirled a lock of hair and picked up a gardening magazine and flicked through the pages, paying zero attention to the articles.

Poor thing. She looked utterly bored. What could he do to cheer her up? Wasn't it what he did all the time? He once borrowed the World Atlas from the library to show Nandini where the island continent of Australia was. One day, he held the logbook while she memorised the sine and cosine of 180 in basic calculus. He'd also helped her make a papier-mâché model of a volcano and showed her the right combination of oil paints and turpentine to create a smooth finish for models of green coconut trees, sandy beaches and the odd turtle or two. Time to try something new.

'Do you know the story of this place?' Karuppan sat opposite Nandini.

She shook her head.

'It's called "The Legend of Nagakanna".'

*

Once upon a time, early in the twentieth century, the colonial managers of Foothills Estate picked up about fifty Tamil indentured labourers from Madras and brought them to tap rubber in the estate.

---

1   Thatch made from palm fronds.

They were given homes and a community developed as their numbers grew. In need of a place of worship, the estate elders commissioned a Hindu priest from Penang to help them locate a suitable place to build a temple. A party of six rubber tappers and the priest spent a month in June roaming the very depths of Foothills Estate.

On the day the Tamils call *pournami*, the day of the full moon, the exhausted priest decided to have a rest. He crouched down by the banks of a river, cupped his hands and scooped up some water to drink. His thirst quenched, he looked up and saw a jasmine tree in full bloom on the islet across the river. Next to the tree, a cobra raised its head and dilated the muscles of its neck to form a hood with a double chevron pattern. It started swaying from side to side.

A dancing snake.

The priest decided that this was a propitious moment and declared the spot a holy one. Everyone agreed that this would be the site of the new temple in Foothills Estate. Once the bridge was constructed, a temple with living quarters for the priest was built on that islet.

The consecration ceremony called *kumbavishaygam* was held soon after. People entered the temple's inner sanctum to place their hopes, prayers, dreams and offerings – gold coins, diamonds or precious stones – in the hollow below a raised platform. The hollow was then sealed and an idol placed above this platform. The entire ceremony was accompanied by continuous recitations of Sanskrit mantras for three days. After this, the temple priest alone entered the inner sanctum. The *kumbavishaygam* was repeated every twelve years.

In the late 1920s, on a cold August morning, the priest heard a loud clanging sound coming from inside the temple. He rushed in to see a man squatting in the middle of the hall clutching his eyes and screaming. A crowbar lay next to him. The priest pulled the man's hands away. What the priest saw, in the light of the kerosene lamp, horrified him: there was blood streaming down the man's cheeks and the sockets of his eyes were empty.

The priest treated the man's wounds and made him rest. Then, he summoned the estate elders. When they arrived, the man confessed that he wanted to steal the jewels and gold in the temple. He had raised the crowbar to strike. Before he could bring it down on the idol, he had heard a hissing sound. The last words the man uttered were, 'I saw the cobra's fangs.'

There was worse to come because he began to run in circles, clutching his ears. He could no longer hear. No one knew his name or where he came from.

The estate elders gave the thief a Tamil name, Nagakanna: 'Naga' meaning 'Cobra' and 'Kanna' meaning 'Eyes'. He spent the remainder of his days in the temple grounds, and the people of Foothills Estate brought him milk and eggs to eat. Within a year, Nagakanna was dead. In spirit form, Nagakanna's sight and hearing were fully restored.

During the next *kumbavishaygam* ceremony, the temple priests had a fright when they discovered a cobra inside the hollow. Two intact eyeballs lay in the centre of its deadly coil. At that moment, a woman in the crowd lay face down on the floor and slithered from side to side, hissing. She was in this trance for no more than five minutes. When it was over, the temple priests looked inside the hollow; the snake and the eyeballs had disappeared. No one knew how the snake got there and no one dared to find out. Henceforth, due reverence was given to this creature and every time there was a religious ceremony in the temple, at least one person in the crowd entered into a trance, slithered and hissed for five minutes.

In time, the children of Foothills Estate grew up, left Sungai Petani and the temple crumbled. The priest's quarters remained, but became dilapidated. And the story of Nagakanna became a frightful legend.

*

Round and round, the bow-legged ghost danced, overjoyed.

Having eavesdropped on Karuppan's narration, he told a slimy baby iguana and a toad, 'I'm a legend, you know. A legend.'

He stopped dancing. 'That bloody cobra.'

Nagakanna blamed the serpent entirely for the loss of his sight, hearing and, eventually, his life. 'If it wasn't for that snake, I'd still be alive. I was looking after my sick mother. I needed money. To buy her medicines.'

The reptile and amphibian lacked the courage to say that, instead of stealing the jewels, he could have prayed for his mother's recovery.

The ghost's excitement vanished when he heard what Nandini said next.

'How can she say that?' He put his hands on his hips, annoyed.

'But how? Not true-lah, this legend.' Nandini pouted.

'And why not?', asked Karuppan in his sing-song voice.

'Karuppan, the cobra's venom is a neurotoxin', she said, rubbing her eyes.

'Wah! Where did you learn such a big word?'

'That's the new word I learned yesterday. It means a poison which acts on the nervous system', Nandini answered.

'Oh', he replied. 'Don't rub your eyes. They're the most important part of the body and the windows to your soul. If you rub them, you can even become blind. Then what? You'll be like Nagakanna – no one knows your name. Your life will be a complete secret.'

Nandini stopped rubbing her eyes, but was quiet. 'I'm not blind. Still, I don't know what my real name is – Nandini or Nadia.'

Karuppan didn't know what to say. There was nothing he could do about the fact that Nandini's father had converted Nandini to Islam without Kamini's consent or knowledge. Even her name was changed to Nadia. He sighed.

'Come', he said and took her hand. 'I have to take you back birthday girl.'

Nandini sighed.

'I suppose so', she said, rubbing her nose.

'What? You don't want a ride on my new motorbike?', he asked.

Nandini's head shot up and she smiled brightly.

'That's better', he said. With his hand on the doorknob, he turned to face her. 'You know, if you become blind, you'll become like this.' He stuck his neck out, and opened his eyes so wide that they bulged.

Nandini burst out laughing.

'That's more like it, Kanna. Be happy', Karuppan said and led her out the front door.

'Look at your mother. She looks so worried', Karuppan said, when they turned into Jalan Sekerat ten minutes later.

Nandini leaned over his shoulder. Kamini stood at the front gates, wringing her hands and pacing. She turned her head when she heard the roar of the motorbike's engine.

'Nandini! Next time you go somewhere, at least tell me first.' Holding her hand out for Nandini, she added, 'Mama is waiting with your birthday cake.'

Nandini took her mother's hand and jumped off the motorbike. 'Thanks, Karuppan.'

He ran a fatherly hand down Nandini's cheek and caught her chin.

'Thanks.' Kamini echoed her child and asked his chin, 'You don't want to come in?'

Sixteen years. And she still won't look at me or say my name.

He looked at Kamini's long hair tied back in one loose plait down her back. Her shoulders in her sleeveless blouse glistened; the contours of her body were deeply attractive. She had become an exotic beauty before his very eyes. He cleared his throat. 'Sorry. I can't.'

Kamini nodded and slid her arm around Nandini's shoulders. Together, they turned, walked into the marquee. He could have stayed a moment longer to watch them and savour the smell of jasmine. Instead, he revved up the engine of his motorbike and rode away.

Ten minutes later, Karuppan threw his keys down on the plastic table at the *mamak* stall opposite the temple. While the hawker fried his *mee goreng*, Karuppan looked at the temple. A boy, with spindly arms and a thin moustache leaned a ladder against the wall. A girl with two plaits down her back stood next to him, holding on to a bunch of fairy lights. Karuppan hoped he didn't make the same mistake. He prayed the boy would say the right thing if the girl confessed her love for him. He looked up at the heavens above and whispered, 'The day she looks me in the eye, I will say I'm sorry.' Touching the scar on his left cheek, he added, 'And that I love her.'

Great-grandmother, Ma

Jennifer Rahim

I remember you
with the scarce economy
that fuels story,

your seldom visits
from down country. Home
was Rio Claro –

an entire town,
the place you journeyed from
unannounced

to children too possessed
by holidays and the sea
to have time for you.

All day you sat like a murti[1]
you never prayed before,
serene and strange

on that one peerah[2]
stationed like a hyphen
in the corridor of a house

that opened at one end
to Point Cumana.
At the other was the ocean

---

1   Image or statue of a Hindu deity.
2   Traditional type of stool.

that delivered you,
a just-budding adolescent
from a ship, its name

long lost to you,
though not the reason
you came –
to marrid he fadda

(the gesture to the son
who wed Africa and settled
on the rim of the Gulf).

Turteen chirren borne
to the Pa, my father remembers
as a quiet man

who spoke a sweet
and secret Hindi with his wife
and became after

the unspoken *before*, a tailor.
A man who loved cinema
for the movies of India –

I was too young
to treasure answers to questions
I never asked;

but I remember you,
a small woman draped in cotton
and sheer, perpetually

pulling an orhni forward,
like a private discipline to forefend
an unspoken return,

more than to cover your hair,
silver, I remember. You
moved in slow music, then.

Wrists chimed and sapatas
tock-tocked around the yard
gathering green leaves;

but I never saw you dance,
never saw the chulha's fire
that perfumed of your clothes.

Your lined face bore
an indecipherable script.

So much never asked,
like your name (you were always,
to me, just Ma).

I bear a name
your son gave to my father,
not really his,

not ever mine;
but I claimed you still. Ma.

You were my own,
in a way. I was never yours
to claim.

Homecoming

Suzanne Bhagan

As they wait in the departure lounge of Beijing airport for the midnight flight, Ravi and Gita notice that the voices have grown louder. A sea of dark faces looms ahead. Chubby bodies clad in garish saris. Lean frames dressed in jeans and untucked shirts opened at the collar. A pot-bellied, middle-aged man wearing a cowboy hat takes a selfie. A woman in a bright yellow shalwar shows another some shiny sandals she has bought. A child clutches a soft, stuffed toy. The glass doors open. They are ready for boarding. The crowds move forward, thick like molasses.

The couple find seats. A nervous man wants the window seat in their row. While waiting for take-off, he speaks loudly on his cell phone. The flight attendant tells him to turn it off. Someone jams Gita's seat from behind. Males cough loudly. The man next to Ravi nibbles on some crumbs from a Ziploc bag.

*

It's their first visit to India. The plane lands terribly. Gita's ears ache. She and Ravi stumble through baggage claim and immigration and then take a pre-paid taxi to the city. It's probably 1.30 am. They leave the protective glass walls of the airport and plunge into the unknown.

The taxi looks like it belongs in the 1960s. It's old and yellow, even vintage-looking. The plastic upholstery is torn and the taxi driver barely speaks English. Ravi and Gita exchange nervous glances.

As the taxi hits the highway, Gita notices the buildings set against the dark sky. Everything looks smeared with moss under the pallid orange street lights. She sees men with prostitutes, wrapped in marijuana tendrils. Two walk briskly along the highway with a silver pot threaded along a bamboo pole between them.

*

Gita can't believe she's in Kolkata. All she knew of the city was that her great-great grandmother got on the ship here for Chinidad, the land of sugar. She had no records, no photographs, only the bare bones of stories her father told her.

130

When she was growing up, home had always been Trinidad, a tiny forgotten rock in the Caribbean Sea. In spite of its physical distance from the motherland, Gita's family had succeeded in creating a little India in their tropical home. They ate Indian food, listened to Indian music and watched Indian movies. Even though her father was a converted Presbyterian, her mother still swept her grandmother's *mandir*[1] in the backyard every week, wiping colourful prints of Hindu gods and goddesses.

Gita and her sister, however, hated being Indian. Every Sunday, their parents would give them plates of curried chicken, dal and rice and make them sit in front of the television to watch a Bollywood movie. It was a weekly ritual: family time and Indian indoctrination.

Three hours later, Gita would be comatose from the heavy dose of the snow-capped Himalayans, heaving bosoms, high-pitched singing, brawls and over-the-top Indian weddings. Afterwards, her parents felt accomplished. Bollywood helped them teach their children how to be good Indians, even in this forgotten corner of the world. Gita and her sister, however, remained beyond instruction. They would rebel and criticise the actresses' makeup and jiggly stomach rolls.

As students of the village's only Presbyterian school, they sneered at the Hindu school on the opposite end of the playing field the two schools shared. Gita and her classmates called the Hindu school students' uniforms 'dal, rice and bhaji' and they labelled the Presbyterian school's red and white uniforms 'red bean and rice'. Creole people food. Yet Gita cringed every lunch time when she took out her roti and vegetable choka sandwich. She never really belonged.

Her father thought it would be a good idea to sign her up for Indian dancing. One Saturday, he took her and her cousin to an Indian dancing school at the edge of the village's cane field. The girls sat at the back, on the concrete lip of a pond filled with goldfish.

'Ta ta, ta ka ke ta ka ke...' the dance instructor droned, clapping the rhythm as his students tapped their feet to the beat. Instead, Gita stared at a stray bell that lay at the bottom of the pond. It was covered by a thin veil of moss. She refused to join the class.

Her cousin caved and soon became the star attraction of their family reunions, always performing dutifully for their relatives.

1   Hindu temple.

'Beautiful dancing!', they whispered, proud that at least one member of the younger generation was interested in their culture. Gita would sulk in the corner, watching her cousin's nimble feet tap across the floor like little palpitating birds.

As Gita got older, she watched more Hollywood movies and read British books. Bollywood's sheen began to crack and fade. The films appeared excessively melodramatic with the over-protective mother, the immovable patriarch, the jealous lover and the vengeful son. When the tragic background music swelled and faces dripped with tears, Gita rolled her eyes.

The Bollywood women were also impossibly beautiful. They all had long, straight hair, pale complexions and graceful bodies. They wore skin-tight bodices and lurid saris that exposed too much bosom, back and stomach. Gita felt sick whenever the camera lingered on their heaving breasts, thrusting hips and *kajal*-rimmed eyes palpitating with sexual desire.

At her girls' high school, her transformation was almost complete. Her teachers encouraged her to study hard and to turn her back on a future as an Indian *dulahin*[2] who cooked roti and touched the husband's feet every morning.

Some of her classmates still remained captive and bleached their dark faces to emulate the Bollywood actresses' milky complexions. They grew their hair long and dyed their straggly strands vermillion and blonde. Instead, eleven-year-old Gita hacked off her thick, long black tresses with a pair of her mother's sewing scissors.

*

The streets grow narrow and winding. The early morning air moistens Gita's face and tangles her hair. A pack of street dogs fight over torn garbage. Men wearing only underwear sleep under a ramshackle roof, their huge pot bellies sunny side up. In another shed, a group of adults and children huddle together on the ground under thin cotton sheets.

Cars constantly honk to overtake the taxi even though the streets are deserted. The sounds carry around the dim corners. The deserted streets never seem to end. Gita wonders, is this the culture capital of India? Home of countless writers, movie directors, Nobel Prize winners? She prays and prays for tall buildings but only sees shacks.

2   Bride or daughter-in-law.

They enter another deserted street. The taxi driver hesitates and slows down. 'No, no, Maria Hotel', Ravi says, keeping his eye on the GPS on his smartphone. The taxi driver doesn't seem to understand. 'Don't stop, not here, not here', he insists, waving his hands to tell the driver to keep moving. The taxi crawls. Gita grabs Ravi's hand. They pull up by a galvanised gate. Above it, Maria Hotel appears in crooked letters.

The security guard looks at them curiously, then takes them to reception. The clerk rubs his eyes. '*Aap kaa naam kyaa hai?*',[3] he asks the two brown faces. Ravi looks confused. Gita quickly says, 'No Hindi.' The clerk seems annoyed. 'No Hindi?', he says under his breath. Gita grits her teeth. Her eyes ache. He shows them to a dirty room and then leaves.

Inside, there is one tiny window blocked by the hotel's generator. The bedsheets and pillowcases are stained with mosquito blood and the smell of sleep. Faulty wiring droops from too many light fixtures, including a green bulb under a chintzy lampshade. The walls are painted a sickly yellow, and there is a giant, chipped patch in one corner. The bathroom ceiling bears the shame of water damage. A few flies buzz noisily.

They turn on the television. A Shah Rukh Khan movie. He and the heroine gambol in lush meadows. But Bollywood had lied. There were no lush meadows in Kolkata.

3 am. Rain falls quietly outside. Gita feels a thick shroud of darkness, dirt and decay envelop her. Ravi gently snores. In the dirty room, she feels as though they've slipped down some dark rabbit hole, a limbo-land of confusion, fear and uncertainty. Gita writes to exorcise the demons already pawing at her ankles. She slips her dirty tee shirt over the smelly pillowcase and covers herself with a pashmina shawl. Already, she feels that India has betrayed them.

*

Something changed in Gita when they moved from Trinidad to China to work. She often felt alone in the staff room. No one spoke to her because she didn't know the language. Men would avoid her fake smile when she held the door open for them.

She started aching to watch Bollywood movies. Gita, who vowed never to become her parents, developed her own ritual. Every night

---

3   'What are your names?'

during winter, she forced Ravi to watch a Bollywood movie with her. Her eyes greedily soaked up the colours on screen. She started singing Bollywood songs in the bathroom. She even started throwing around Hindi words whenever she spoke to Ravi. 'I don't know why but I much prefer Hindi to Mandarin. I just get it', she said. Ravi just shook his head. After watching too many movies, Gita suddenly felt a pang in her stomach. She had to go to India.

*

Day 2. Ravi and Gita barricade themselves in their room. They seek refuge in American sitcoms they used to watch in Trinidad: *The Big Bang Theory, America's Funniest Videos*. They fall asleep again. Gita gets up, feeling claustrophobic. Their water supply is running low. They have to go outside even though Gita doesn't want to.

The sky is grey; the air choked with car exhaust fumes and the sweet scent of tobacco. The sidewalks of CIT Road are wet and filthy, covered with dead leaves and bits of garbage. All the shop fronts are shuttered. Ladies' Park, a nondescript patch of green, lies opposite the hotel. There are no tall buildings, no foreigners. Just empty cabs parked along a dirty, nondescript street in a forlorn, forgotten city. Pedestrians look harried, poor and resigned. A group of old men sit on the pavement playing cards. The cars continue to honk mercilessly. Gita has seen enough and refuses to venture past the street corner.

*

Day 3. They venture outside again but stay within the safety of the hotel's driveway. Ravi introduces himself to one of the staff. His name is Kaushik. A very Calcutta name, he says. His mother is dead and he has a father and one sister. She's married with two children. He is single.

In Ladies' Park, men play cricket, their bats flailing high over their heads. Ravi and Kaushik start talking about it. Kaushik knows about the Jamaican Tallawahs and Chris Gayle but has never heard about Trinidad.

'Are you Indian?', he asks tentatively.

'No, we're from Trinidad', Ravi explains.

'Canada? But you look Indian...', he insists.

Gita watches feral dogs tear wet napkins on the sidewalk. The streets are busier now, heaving with buses, scooters, motorcycles and cars. The buses are crammed with humanity and barely stop to empty passengers. People hop on and off while it continues to move. A woman balances sideways on the back of a scooter. Her slippered feet dangle carelessly over the open road. Traffic moves fast yet no one falls, trips, loses their balance or smashes into anything. A thin thread of order holds the apparent chaos together, keeping it from unravelling.

Gita looks at the trees in the park. They seem ill, choked by car fumes. Their leaves are straggly and their branches offer little shade. Men swagger by in jeans and long-sleeved plaid shirts. Women scurry by, their heads covered, their eyes downcast, their faces devoid of any makeup. Gita searches for the beautiful, fair faces she saw in Bollywood movies. She searches for her own face in the teeming crowds but sees none.

Back in the room, the lights go off. Infinite darkness. Fear grows in the middle of Gita's throat and begins to rise. Her breaths get shallow. She grabs Ravi's hands and asks him to pray as tears stream down her face. Kolkata scares her. She wishes she was back in Trinidad, even China. Why did she come to this God-forsaken place?

*

Day 4. It's Gita's birthday today. She's thirty-two. They go to the city centre to get rupees. Pedestrians saunter across the street even when traffic's coming at full speed, fluttering their palms up down to slow down. In the middle of the street, someone's hung laundry. The taxi passes one decrepit building after another. In front of a Catholic school, a sign reads, 'No horn please' yet the horns continue to bray.

There are more signs: English lessons, mathematics lessons, physics lessons. Just like in Trinidad. The road is filled with potholes like open sores. Just like in Trinidad.

The dusty tram runs on tracks parallel to the main street, crammed with people. Motorcycles slip in and out of spaces. A feral dog stands in front of a modern cake shop. There is no quiet in this city. People wear haggard faces. A man prays to an orange statue. The flower garlands in front of a shop's entrance are covered in dust. Gita smells something familiar: incense and popcorn.

They stop at the market. Gita clutches her bag protectively, covering it with her shawl. People rush past. They have to cross the street. Gita feels tears welling up. The traffic races forward. Ravi takes her hand and they dart across the street like everyone else.

No one wants to change their dollars. In the banks, the Indians are cleaner, fairer and more beautiful. How do they go to and from work every day in the face of such decrepitude? The bank clerks look puzzled when they see Ravi and Gita's sweaty Indian faces speaking a strange, accented English. They seem incongruous, as though they should belong but don't.

A man in the West Bengal Tourism Office tells them to go to the next building to find a foreign exchange kiosk. 'What's the name of the building?', Gita asks. 'Go to the next building', he repeats and turns away.

They continue walking. The pavement occasionally smells of shit or urine. Sometimes, there's a pile of excrement on the wet sidewalk. There are no flowers like in Trinidad. The pavement tiles are uneven and broken in places. There are packs of street dogs with short-haired coats, curly tails and pointy ears. They look rough. At least in Trinidad, the dogs seemed harmless. These Kolkata dogs scare Gita.

As they look for the kiosk, they pass Kolkata's monuments: the church spires that seem to belong to London and colonial-style buildings, crushed by neglect and time. It's as though the British completely abandoned the city when India declared its independence. The past remains, while humans scurry about the ruins like rats. No one ever looks up. There's no sun in the grey, cloud-choked sky. Gita wonders, how do these people motivate themselves to escape this hellhole? How did her ancestors ever get the courage to leave?

They pass the Writer's Building. As a child, Gita discovered that she loved to rhyme. She would spend afternoons after school, going through the entire alphabet looking for the right sound. She even compiled her poems in a little yellow book. Once, her cousin borrowed it to show to one of their teachers. She never gave it back. It remained somewhere in the school or was probably thrown away. Gita was crushed.

She also remembers meeting a woman in church who was a poet living in Canada.

'Just write', she said, 'Just write.'

*

Gita is getting hungry. They pass vendors selling green guavas flecked with water drops, big yellow slices of pineapple perfumed with burning incense to drive away the flies. Another stall sells stale, technicolour Indian sweets.

They still haven't got rupees. Rain starts to drizzle. She crumples in defeat and refuses to cross any more streets. Miraculously, Ravi spots the foreign exchange kiosk. There it is, just two buildings away from the tourism office. Gita curses loudly. The kiosk is closed. She's ready to leave this dump of a city and India.

Then a man appears. At first he appears reluctant but eventually changes all their dollars to rupees. 'Sorry madam', he says, closing the door while he and Ravi count the bills inside the kiosk. They appear to be speaking like old friends. Gita stands outside the booth, sweaty, hungry and tired.

*

Day 5. Outside the hotel, humanity pours from every hole, every corner, every crevice. Everyone looks busy doing something to survive: begging, selling, washing, scurrying, like animals in a cage. Busy, but with no real direction.

*

Day 6. Ravi and Gita walk through Kolkata's side streets teeming with young schoolgirls. The girls wear blue skirts and white shirts and squeal while running along the haphazardly tiled pavement. One girl holds a piece of Bristol board with bits of cotton stuck on it. A group crams into a jeep and speed off, chattering excitedly.

Seeing the excited girls makes Gita remember. Post-9/11. One hundred-plus girls dressed in varying shades of pastel blue file into a humid auditorium to the familiar strains of 'Pomp and Circumstance'. As graduates, they sit on chairs, not on the terrazzo floor *pundit*-style as they had always done before.

When their names are called, the girls subtly detach dresses that cling to their womanly hips, buttocks and thighs. They walk to the podium to collect their certificates, worried about whether these dresses are translucent in the harsh mid-morning light. They look different in new makeup and elaborate updos. They are glad to leave a school that looks good on their resumés but, secretly, they delight in the freedom of being able to hang out with boys without being shamed for not behaving like 'young ladies'.

Gita is one of those girls in the ocean of pastel blue. She receives the prizes, accolades for being the good girl who always did her homework and a little extra. However, she is unsure. Expectations weigh on her shoulders. The world is now wide open.

*

Ravi and Gita go to the newest mall in Kolkata. The glass revolving doors are clean. The tiled floor shines. Some stores are still closed: Gucci, Tumi, Burberry and Swarovski. The mall seems alien: clean, sanitised, quiet and serene. They sit in a coffee shop. An Indian man behind them says, '*Aak* cappuccino', then chats to two women in fluid English. The women twitter like little birds.

Ravi and Gita go to a clothing store. The attendant, a middle-aged woman, is curious. 'Where are you from?', she asks. 'West Indies', Ravi says. Soon, her conversation erupts into criticisms about foreigners and non-resident Indians (NRIs) who only take pictures of the slums in Kolkata. 'Every country has slums. Even China has slums but they moved them all out of Beijing before the Olympics.'

She talks about the rich NRIs who return to Kolkata to buy cheap clothes to sell back in their adopted countries. 'You know the ones who like to flaunt their riches. They love to come for Durga *puja*[4] and buy stuff then fly out.'

Ravi tells her that they used to live in China. She doesn't seem impressed. 'I was there. All I ate was bread and fruits like a monkey. Don't they know that not everyone wants to eat frogs and snakes?' Gita smiles awkwardly.

*

Gita and Ravi head to Victoria Memorial. In the garden, weeds grow unruly and thick. It's unbearably sticky and hot. The front of the monument is impressive enough: great chunks of white marble hewn into domes, angels, lions and a life-sized replica of a corpulent English queen sitting atop her throne.

---

4   Annual Hindu festival in celebration of the goddess Durga.

Gita rests on a bench near the only fan in the building. Two guards shoo her off. They casually hold ancient-looking guns and expressions of self-importance. They take their places on the bench in front of the fan.

Ravi and Gita then walk to St Paul's Cathedral. The white building streaked with age hides behind cool trees. Inside the church, it is completely silent. Suspended ceiling fans rotate like small plane propellers. Five-petalled flowers adorn the ceiling. At their feet are benches covered in torn leather. Sunlight streams through the murky yellow-and-green stained-glass windows. As they leave the compound, a light-brown street dog stops and wags its tail. Gita cries inside. It's the first time she's truly felt welcome in the city.

*

Day 7. Dawn. They leave today. Kolkata is waking up. In the hotel garage, Gita hears the radio playing an old Bollywood song she vaguely remembers. Her chest fills with pain and nostalgia. They hop in a taxi for the airport. A truck filled with crates of live chickens passes them. The air is cool.

On the left, the taxi driver points at two buildings with a swimming pool wedged between them and shop fronts for Porsche, BMW and Benz. A sign for an ice-skating rink. Education fair: Study in Australia. A new mall under construction. Salt Lake Stadium. On the right, a line of shacks. A woman brushes her teeth with her finger. A group of men douse themselves, clad in wet dhotis.

The taxi careens forward, sailing through a clutch of trucks, cars, buses, rickshaws and motorcycles. Billboards of an artist painting *kajal* on a goddess's slanted eyes. Another of the goddess's red-stained feet.

In the air, Kolkata looks benign: a patchwork of cheerful pink, peach, orange and yellow buildings. None of the squalor shows through. Further afield, condos and hotels and the brown Hooghly river snakes along placidly. Gita sighs. India had stripped them slowly, piece by piece. They just didn't know why yet.

139

Erased

Athol Williams

He swatted at my question with the morning *Times*
rolled up tight. His brow like cobras uneasily lying
side by side. He looked up at me, above his glasses,
left corner of his mouth hooked up. Sweat boulders
hurried down his face, as if to escape some horror
in his memory.
                    Where do we come from Daddy?

Swing, swipe the newspaper baton went, a swatter
at imaginary everywhere flies in summer's flames.
He cursed my intrusion of his peace, and the sun's
intrusion of his shade, and my question's dusting
of his suitcase of hidden pain.

He lied like a colonial judge but I knew the truth –
I could smell the boiling rice and milk of Pongal,
overflowing with jaggery[1] and cashews and raisins,
I could hear the priests blow their conch shells, I
could feel the clickety-clackety heartbeat of a train
in my veins, that train that rumbled from the slums
of Madras with its cargo of dreams into purgatory,
the miles of the Indian Ocean salty with the tears
of our grandmothers, to the labour camps of Natal's
sugar plantations, to Transvaal's gold mines, to the
empty tables at the foot of Cape Town's mountain.

One day he showed me a map of India:
                    See, there is no Madras!

But I knew the truth – Madras was erased, wiped
from the map, like our dreams, like our house in
District Six, erased, like our name, our tongue.

1   Coarse dark-brown sugar.

Famished Eels[1]

Mary Rokonadravu

I

After one hundred years, this is what I have: a daguerreotype of her in bridal finery; a few stories told and retold in plantations, kitchens, hospitals, airport lounges. Scattered recollections argued over expensive telephone conversations across centuries and continents by half-asleep men and women in pyjamas. Arguments over mango pickle recipes on email and private messages on Facebook. A copper cooking pot at the Fiji Museum. Immigration passes at the National Archives of Fiji. It is 2011.

Fiji, with Guyana, Suriname and Trinidad and Tobago, has just registered the 'Records of the Indian Indentured Labourers' into the UNESCO Memory of the World Register, when my father, the keeper and teller of stories, suffers a stroke. Fate has rendered his tongue silent. He cannot read or write – he first set foot in a classroom at fifteen, and was told by a nun he was too old. He ignores my journalist and doctor siblings to select me, the marine biologist, to finish his task. I am off the coast of Lifou in New Caledonia counting sea urchins when the call is relayed.

He hates me for not becoming a journalist, I say to myself.

I will be on the Thursday flight, I tell my older sister.

She meets me at the airport and drives me down to Suva. It is past midnight. We pass eleven trucks overloaded with mahogany logs between Nadi and Sigatoka. A DHL courier truck. A quiet ambulance. She smokes at the wheel, flicking ash into the cold highway wind. We pass a dim lamp-lit wooden shack before we reach Navua. Someone is frying fish. We both know it is fresh cod. We remain silent as we are flung into the kitchen of our childhood at Brown Street in Toorak. We stop to sip sweet black tea from enamel pialas in Navua.

---

1   Previously published in *Granta* magazine, 28 April 2015.

Come on tell me, she blurts. Who you seeing now? Is it a dark-skinned Kanak?[2] Is that what's keeping you in Lifou? Do you speak French now?

Screw you, I say from the back seat.

He wants you to do this because you won't lie to him, she says. The rest of us may. Just to make him happy. Just give him what he wants to hear. But you won't. You will find out and you will tell him.

Screw you, I say again, more to myself than her.

All his life, my father has sought one thing only – to know the woman in the photograph. To know the name of her city or town in India. To know that at some juncture in history, there was a piece of earth he could call his own. All he had had was a lifetime of being told he was *boci. Baku. Taga vesu.* Uncircumcised.

A hundred years was not enough. Another five hundred would not be either. In a land where its first peoples arrived a couple of thousand years before the first white man, the descendants of indenture would forever remain weeds on a forsaken landscape. A blight.

He had stubbornly remained in Fiji through three military coups and one civilian takeover. Everyone had left. He remained the one who rented out flats until his brothers' houses were sold. He supervised brush-cutting boys on hot Saturday mornings. He was the one to call the plumber to change faucets in grimy, unscrubbed shower recesses. He was the one who kept receipts for oil-based butternut paint, bolts and drill bits; photocopied them faithfully at the municipal library and mailed them to Australia, Canada or New Zealand. Each envelope had a paper-clipped note: OK. It was the only word he learned to write. I received Christmas cards from him saying the same thing: OK. The handwriting on the envelope changed depending on who the postmaster was at the time.

His younger brothers send out family newsletters by email. They always use the same photograph of my father, a blurred profile of him holding a beer, with the same caption – 'Still refuses to use email.' I wish to click Reply All and say fuck you but there is a distant niece in Saskatchewan on the list – she writes me regularly for shark postcards and she knows the scientific names of eleven types of

2   Indigenous Melanesian inhabitants of New Caledonia, southwest Pacific.

nudibranch. She recorded herself reciting it like bad poetry and put it on YouTube. I am the only one who knows this. She insists I use real handwriting, real stamps. She hates pancakes, frogs, flatlands. Her handwriting yearns for water. Salt water. Sea. In her milk-tooth grin I see the next storyteller – the one to replace the man who has gone silent. She is ten and wants three pet octopi.

I was born to be a bridge. All I see are connections. I bridge between time, people and places. I study migratory species. Tuna fish stocks. Whales. Sea urchins in between. Cephalopods. I was nine when I picked up my first cuttlefish bone on a tidal flat in Pacific Harbour. For years I thought it was a whistle. I wrote out the names of the world's oceans, seas, currents and fish in longhand, unaware the lead scrawlings were placing miles between my father and me. He watched me from across the kitchen table. My mother had died bringing me into the world. He washed okra with patient fingers. Boiled rice. Warned me he was going to slice red onions.

Make sure you buy land, he whispers. When you grow up, buy a small piece of land. Build a house just for you. Promise me.

I promised. But my eyes were already on the Kuroshio Current. I was already reading the voyage of Captain James Cook and the transit of the planet Venus. Hearing the howl of winds at Tierra del Fuego. No one told me that as recently as one hundred years before, ships had cut through the rough straits with people carrying the makings of my teeth in their genes. They almost never happened. Almost.

Keep writing, he says in our old kitchen. As long as someone remembers, we live.

My sister drops me off at the Colonial War Memorial Hospital.

I won't come in now, she says. I still smell of cigarettes.

My father is asleep when I reach out to hold his hand.

II

For years the story in my family was that she boarded a ship in Calcutta. After all, it was the holy city of pilgrimage. It was nice to believe I descended from the loins of a young devotee travelling north to immerse in the sacred Ganges. She was then kidnapped and sent to labour in the hot sugar-cane regions of Fiji. She had hair the sheen of sea-washed rocks at dusk. The story was that she met

Narayana on the ship, the son of a turmeric merchant. They were to have eleven children of which only two survived, one of them my father's father, Venkat.

I grew up imagining the digging of little graves at the edge of sugar-cane. In rain. It was always night rain, as if miscarriages or infant deaths only occurred in rain-drenched darkness. In childhood, I added details from Bollywood films to it: night wailing, tugs-of-war over linen-swaddled baby corpses. Murder. Narayana strangles his own children. He uses an old cotton sari. There was no photograph of him, so in my mind he wore the face of the Bollywood villain, Amjad Khan. Rewind a few years to the port of Calcutta and the ship that crossed the *kala pani*, the black waters, and he is Amitabh Bachchan. He was the designated toilet-water carrier on the ship to Fiji – this much was whispered behind hushed curtains at home. At celebrations he is remembered as an astrologer, squinting his face at the heavens, reading palms on a heaving sea. He reads prosperity into suicidal hands, keeps men and women breathing until landfall. He has not created life yet. Nor ended any.

There is no photograph of him. But there is the one photograph of her. She is sitting rigid under a cascade of jewellery. For years, no one asked what a virgin devotee was doing with so much gold or with a nose ring that could collar a grown cat.

Now it comes to me.

III

My father's house, the new one, is by the banks of the Rewa River, directly opposite the township of Nausori, a rice-growing region of wetland and rain. He has a concrete house on a slight knoll. A sprawling pumpkin out back. He can see the old bridge from his kitchen sink. He has seen at least six women leap to their deaths from that bridge. The last one dropped two toddlers and a baby first. The Nausori Police Station knows his telephone number. A cleaning-woman comes in twice a week. I am told all this by his neighbour, a buxom Fijian woman who leads her children in loud, charismatic prayers before dawn. She sells pineapple and custard pies outside MH Supermarket and sings soprano at the New Spring Church Choir.

I put my bags in the living room. It is full of books and newspapers. There are boxes of printed emails, audio-cassette recordings, photographs and signed copies of diasporic books by names such as

Brij Lal, Mohit Prasad, Sudesh Mishra and Subramani. My father has been attending numerous poetry readings and lecture series at the universities. There was an invitation to a film premiere in Ba and one to a wedding in Labasa. He has been listening to *ghazals*[3] I bought as a Christmas gift for him on Amazon. He was chopping tomatoes when he collapsed. Jagjeet and Chithra Singh were still singing when my sister walked in with a pot of duck curry.

He is so happy you're here, she says in the hospital corridor. I told him you're going to look at his boxes of research. I know he is happy.

My sister has showered and washed out the smell of cigarettes from her mouth. She watches the rain pouring out of the hospital's clogged guttering.

Do you think you can tell him about the photograph? Let him know who we are?

IV

My earliest memory of a story is my father's about eels. He is the oldest among his brothers. The only one not in school. He loves books, particularly books without pictures. He loves the smell of wood and dried binding glue in books. He loves cloth-bound books. More than anything, he loves the swirl and fixed width of ink, of typefaces, of fonts readers decipher like enigmatic mysteries. His youngest brother, Mohandas, now a retired pot-bellied plumber in Brisbane, Australia, is seven the year my father discovers eels.

My father grows and harvests rice. He keeps ducks that feed on tadpoles, fry and elvers. My father traps eels to eat the year the rice crop is destroyed by two cyclones. He makes a deal with Mohandas. He gives his share of eel cutlets to Mohandas in exchange for books being read to him.

My father goes without meat for about a year. Then a spell of dry weather sets in. The sky is cloudless. The sun, scorching. The rice paddies dry up into little pools of muck. On a routine walk around the fields he encounters his first writhing frenzy of eels. They have congregated into diminishing pools of water. He watches the large eels kill and eat the smaller ones. He empathises with small eels. He learns to clean and roast eels on an open fire. He trusses them with

---

3   Lyric poems with a fixed number of verses and a repeated rhyme, often on the theme of love.

a guava twig from mouth to tail. He fills his belly and takes home enough to go around twice. It turns out to be a good year.

He tells us we are like eels in a decreasing pool of rain. That we must work hard to buy land in another country.

What does it matter? I remember saying. We will always be the ones who arrived later.

You will be a new, young eel, he says. You will not feel as much pain for a world you have yet to love. You will be the famished eel. Hungry until death. I pray you find a black cloud to give you rain.

That's a horrible story, I say.

His laughter fills the orange-lit afternoon.

Yet now, here he lies silent. I place my fingers on his wrist. I feel my father's floating and hollow pulse, what the Chinese call the scallion stalk pulse. It is said to grace the wrists of those who have suffered massive bleeding. My father has bled all his life. I know the scallion stalk pulse has been a long time coming.

I do what I have not done in years.

I talk to God.

V

I knew years ago that my father knew I knew about the woman in the photograph, our elusive ancestor. He knows I am the researcher he taught me to be. He knows the path of relentless questions he first placed me upon. He knew this from the days of vegetable cleaning and fish chopping in the little kitchen in Toorak. He knew I knew when I stopped coming home. As a fellow traveller, he respected my path and my stance. I followed whale pods across the Tonga Trench the first Christmas away.

You will grow into your road, he tells me when I am a child. And I have.

The archives tell me she arrived in Fiji on the SS *Jumna* at thirteen. Her name is Vellamma. She is treated for a sexually transmitted infection off the coast of Africa. She is the cause of four brawls on board the SS *Jumna*, during one of which three coolies fall overboard, unable to be rescued. Coolies – that's what the records called them.

She has liaisons with more than ten men before she is put into the lines at Rarawai. She kills the first eight of her children. There are inconclusive police and court records. She keeps a daughter alive. The one daughter is taken in by the Methodist Church in Toorak the year Vellamma is imprisoned for the brutal murder of a Muslim man by the name of Talat Mahmoud.

By the time I have uncovered this story, I have sat through hours adding up to days and nights, weeks and months, at the National Archives, hunched over both public and private records. I make copies of numerous photographs of her. I make copies of the only photograph of her daughter, at about eleven years old, acting Mother of Jesus at the Dudley Orphanage Christmas play. She has my father's eyes. She will bear him more than a decade down the line. She will fall in love with a Madrasi pot-seller who will drown on a clear blue day in a clear blue lagoon. For now, she looks alarmed at the camera.

VI

I am five the year my father tells me how to tell a story.

Always make room for uncertainty, he says. Don't say someone said this or said that. Don't ever be sure. Just walking from this kitchen to the backyard you will lose what I have just told you. Make room for that.

My father teaches me the accountability of self-questioning reported speech. I have always made room. We all make room in different ways. My father edits his stories according to who is listening.

I leave for fear of telling the truth. I leave for fear of telling untruths. I leave for fear of not providing enough room in the parentheses I place at the juncture of words and stories. My story is not mine alone. It is the story of multitudes and it will become a thread in the stories of multitudes to come.

If, according to my father, I can lose truth between the kitchen and the backyard, imagine the chasms of separation demarcated by clocks and geographies, between oceans and sleeps. Between lives eating grilled okra at one table. A cat laying his fur on a warm stone. My sister calling him for a fish-head treat. My playing this very scene in my head eighteen years later on a reef in New Caledonia when I receive the news that my father wishes to see me.

VII

My sister fights the afternoon traffic to pick me up from my father's house in Nausori. I have a folder of papers and photographs in a satchel. I will tell my father about Vellamma and Naranya. I have reprints of photographs of Madras under the British Raj. I have photographs of the SS *Jumna*. I have reprints of immigration passes. I have death certificates. I have the photograph of a copper cooking pot.

But, more importantly, I have three handwritten letters from the distant niece growing among the wheat fields of Saskatchewan. Today, I wish him to meet her. A new storyteller who is yet to grow into her road, which will bring her to the edge of British Columbia, to the Pacific coast of Canada. Today, I watched her recite nudibranch names on YouTube. I closed my eyes on the fifth rerun. This girl is coming home.

I listen to her growing hunger. This eel will find the great expanse of Saskatchewan too small for her. Her hunger will bring her home to the sea. The Pacific will be her black cloud.

At the roundabout in Nakasi my sister stops to refuel. I walk into the Hot Bread Kitchen to buy two cream buns. My sister and I will eat these as we head into Laucala Beach Estate, before the turn-off into Vatuwaqa and Flagstaff. I realise I have missed family. My sister licks her thumb and asks for a tissue. She has sugar grains on her nose.

At the hospital, my father is behind pea-green hospital curtains. The nurses have covered him. His body is growing cold. My sister has held him tightly to herself for me. She has not wept. She has not called his brothers. She has made me pack my stories into a satchel just as when we were children. She will hold my hand as we walk outside.

You do realise, she will say, it is you who will keep these stories after Daddy?

She eases the car into the hospital parking lot. I see the sun caught in a wisp of her hair. We are two eels. Famished. Our black cloud awaits.

I have yet to find out as I hand her the tissue for the sugar on her nose.

Rights of Passage

Patti-Anne Ali

a three-part journey

Part 1

She stands before him
proudly humble
memories of mother's milk
a fleeting instant on child-like lips
averting eyes of blatant beauty
dark-lashed, earth-brown and almond-shaped
from his elderly, lustfully wheezing gaze.
This place of warm, muddy cows
and powerful rivers
shrill cries of ancient devotion
travelling on gentle breezes
has suddenly
become her jail
and her mother's voice
an Executioner's song.
He jingles of money
her family's saviour
who will wrench her forever
from sun-drenched fields
of innocence and laughter.
She
is eight years old
and about to marry…

Part 2

Flames rise and grow
consuming the wood
ferociously.
She feels the heat
through the thin material
that rubs
one last time
against her cringing flesh.
She watches
his age-old body
through the folds of cloth
and billows of bitters-sweet smoke
as flames leap and work their way insidiously
reaching for her.
With pounding heart
seized with terror
zombie-like
she is led to the pyre
and submits screaming
to an agony of tradition.
She is twenty-three
and
about to die...

Part 3

Rising from the ashes
of her husband's funeral pyre
she floats
through time and space
over continents and seas
and after a rocky voyage

on a turbulent, tossing vessel
she lands on the shores of an unchartered land.
Through cane and pain
she dances
her body
the epitome of woman
the pinnacle of motherhood
hips that sway in a timeless dance of light
hips that house the children
slumbering peacefully in her
ample curves.
She dances to the island thump
of a drum called the tassa.
This land feeds her new food
strokes her tumbling cascade of
black hair
with the softest of fragrant, tropical breezes
and introduces her to another
whose hair
is not like hers
and another
whose eyes are not like hers
and another whose skin is not like hers.
Her elders frown
as she gambols playfully
with the others.
But they cannot stop her now.
She is too far ahead
shoulder to shoulder with the
others of this new world
doing things she never did before
and things she has done, since time immemorial
gathering her children beneath her protective gaze
gathering policies to implement her destiny.
The elders

rumble in discontent
pretend she does not exist.
She smiles at her Executioners
choosing to remember
warm, muddy cows and powerful rivers
shrill cries of ancient devotion
travelling on gentle breezes.
She reaches within
for what was born centuries ago
in ancestors
who bled and struggled, loved and lived
and breathes a prayer of gratitude
for these timeless gifts
she will pass onto her children
born in this land
that celebrates the shimmer of her tears
in the light of the sun
and illumines her brightly bejewelled figure
poised
on the threshold of discovery
love
firmly planted in this soil.
She has righted her passage.
She has chosen her luggage.
She voyages on.

The Protest March that Ended Indian Indentureship in St Vincent

Arnold N. Thomas

St Vincent and the Grenadines lies a hundred miles west of Barbados and north of Trinidad and Tobago. It has a population of some 120,000 comprised of Africans, Caribs, Europeans, Portuguese Madeirans, as well as Indians, who number around 6,500. Between 1861 and 1880 eight ships brought 2,474 Indians to St Vincent as indentured workers; however, by 1884, 1,141 had returned to their homeland. This essay examines the experience of indentured Indians in St Vincent and the conditions that led to the end of indentureship.

Living and working conditions

When clearance was given by the Colonial Office to bring in Indians, the St Vincent planters specifically requested Calcutta Indians since, in the Caribbean, Indians from the southern Madras region had a reputation for being prone to violence and for disrespecting laws and estate managers. But it was only South Indians that, in 1861, boarded the ships for St Vincent and, when the *Travancore* dropped anchor in Edinboro on 1 June of that year, it was carrying 260 of them, two more than the number with which it had left port Madras, for there had been two births and no deaths, something absolutely remarkable in the annals of the transportation of Indians. The South Indians exceeded all expectations and became model workers for those who followed them later, including workers from northern India.

Their fortunes very much depended on the fortunes of the estate, for example the price of sugar had fallen and the island was being hit by bad weather when the second shipload of Indian workers arrived in 1862. Under those circumstances planters attempted to cut costs by lowering wages and withdrawing the customary weekly allowances of molasses, rum and sugar. About 200 workers at the Mt Bentinck estate protested the manager's move by stopping all operations there on 22 September1862. From then until October the 'molasses riots' spread southwards on several estates reaching four miles to the east of Kingstown.

When the second ship *Castle Howard* arrived in 1862, conditions were so bad that the planters refused to take up their allotments and the 300 or so Indians had to be housed at military barracks in the capital, Kingstown. The treasury had to pay a really high price for their upkeep before they left for the estates.

The prime targets of the rioters were unquestionably the planters and managers, but immigrants were also targeted. Portuguese shops were looted, for example, and Indians were forced off the fields by blacks at several estates. However, local newspaper *St. Vincent Guardian* reported, on 18 November 1865, that, unlike St Lucia, 'our coolie venture is a successful one', citing the presence of Indian indentured labourers as a stimulant to native workers, who turned out in large numbers on many estates after they had been introduced. In addition, Indians were noted for being thrifty, hardly ever committing a crime, and for baptising their children as Christians.

Over the next decades, five ships arrived from Calcutta bringing a total of 1,700 Indians to St Vincent. Each ship was greeted with much fanfare as heralding a new era of prosperity and good relations between workers and employers. But when the first group of thirty-five Indians returned to the home country in 1871, they complained that they had received less than their contract wage of ten pence per day and, as a result, the Indian government gave low priority to emigration to St Vincent. It was not until 1874 that labour emigration resumed, prompted by severe famines in India and by a new Immigration Act in 1874.

The last ship to bring Indians to St Vincent was the *Lightning*, which arrived on the island on 22 May 1880 with 213 of them. The *Lightning* also carried a consignment of Indians for Jamaica. By then, the international market for sugar had become highly competitive and there were indications (based on falling export statistics) that, with its low-grade muscovado sugar, St Vincent could not hope to compete internationally.

Deteriorating social conditions

As had happened so many times before in adverse economic conditions, planters sought to cut costs which inevitably meant cutting wages, increasing tasks and, in the case of the Indians, neglecting their obligations to them under the law. In August 1882, the acting administrator, Roger Tuckford Goldsworthy, received eighty-two complaints from Indians alleging ill-treatment, non-payment of wages and other abuses. Alarmed by the regularity of the complaints, he reported the matter to Governor Robinson, who immediately ordered an investigation. This was conducted by R.P. Cropper from St Lucia. The Cropper Inquiry resulted in a report that catalogued the wretched living and working conditions on all twenty-three estates employing Indian workers. It included notes on the prevalence of diseases such as yaws and tubboes,[1] which had not been brought from India, and the failure of all officials concerned with the administration of the indenture system, which had clearly broken down.

The march on Kingstown: the watershed in the indenture experience

The Cropper Inquiry did not make life easier for the Indians, indeed it led to the reverse: they were treated more harshly as economic conditions worsened, and in October 1882 another attempt was made to reduce their wages while squeezing more work out of them.

For years the much-maligned Indian was caricatured as the weak and feeble 'coolie', always cowering before anyone in authority, too scared to speak up for his rights, let alone fight back. That image was shattered when the Indians at Argyle Estate decided to protest about its management. On 7 October 1882, fifty of them downed cutlass[2] and hoe and marched all the way to Kingstown in defiance of the manager, Mr McKenzie, and also of the laws of St Vincent, in order to bring their grievances directly to the lieutenant governor. Imagine the sight of fifty barefooted Indians leaving Argyle Estate. On their way to Kingstown, ten miles away, they were joined by more Indians from other estates, and for the first time in its history Kingstown was crammed with protesters – and they were all Indians. This was the first recorded protest march by labourers of any kind in St Vincent; previous protests by estate workers had taken the form of strikes and riots on the estates themselves. The Indians had crossed a new threshold in their relations with the estate and government

---

1   Painful sores, mainly between the skin and flesh of the soles of the feet.
2   The main tool used by indentured cane-cutters.

authorities. The protest march was not only against abuses and loss of wages, but also against unfulfilled contractual arrangements. Many of those taking part were from the ill-fated *Countess of Ripon*, which had sunk off Barbados on 20 January 1866; the survivors alleged that they had been cheated out of their return passage, a promise they expected to be fulfilled, despite them having laboured under indenture for as long as sixteen years. They were marching to the governor to make him aware of the promise to return them to India after fulfilment of their contracts.

On reaching the capital, seven of the Indians – one of them a superintendent on the estate – were identified as ringleaders and promptly arrested on the criminal charge of vagabondism, having left the estate without permission, and having gone beyond the two-mile limit. The 'Argyle 7' – Gunga Persad, Dhumar, Puttoolawl, Bhogroo, Rampersad, Kallideen and Saba Singh – were brought before the police magistrate and found guilty of vagrancy or vagabondism. The Indians received little support, not even from Nassaw Forster, the protector of Indians. George Smith, a local attorney, was the only one to speak on their behalf, but to no avail. The Indians felt that everyone in authority was hostile to them.

Response of the Colonial Office and end of indentureship

The decision was a bitter blow to the Indians and thereafter many of them, feeling they were no longer needed in St Vincent, wanted to leave. Two months later, with the assistance of George Smith, a petition was forwarded to the Colonial Office, on behalf of the seven Indians from the *Countess of Ripon*, alleging that they had been deprived of their right of return passage. If anyone had thought of making St Vincent their permanent home, their hopes had been dashed by the decision against the 'Argyle 7'. Surprisingly, the Colonial Secretary of State conceded that an injustice had been done and issued instructions to restore the right to a return passage, not only to the seven petitioners but also to other survivors of the ill-fated ship, who had served equally long and wished to return to India. To meet the high cost of repatriation for such a large group, a Royal Commission visiting in 1883 recommended giving lands to the Indians in lieu of the £10 bounty, but planters refused to sell lands lying idle, while the local administration claimed that little Crown land was available.

Soon after the protest march, the colonial administration was confused about the number actually entitled to return passage because of the protector's sloppy record-keeping. The state of affairs became so bad that, by 1884, estates no longer wanted any Indians, whether indentured or free, living on them. Faced with that situation, Lieutenant Governor Gore even considered deporting them all to Demerara or Trinidad.

The Colonial Office's response to deteriorating conditions on the island was a directive to send all Indians back to India if they could not find work and a home to live, which resulted in many of them registering to return to their home country.

During May and August 1885, 554 Indians departed for India. Many more, crowding into Kingstown, wanted to return, but for whatever reason were not registered. On 1 August 1885, Kingstown was again crammed with Indians as the last ship *The Bruce* prepared to depart for their home country. The 327 registered to return were assembled in the police barracks and, as their names were called, passed through two lines of police to the boats to be ferried out to the waiting ship. This procedure ensured that no Indian wishing to return, but not registered, would slip through the police cordon to the vessel.

On board, the returnees were given new clothes, caps, *lotahs* (dishes), combs and mirrors, and the men received razors, farewell gifts from the St Vincent government which were all they had to show for their long, hard labour. In all, of the 2,474 who had gone to St Vincent, 1,141 returned to India because they could see no future prospect on the island.

Interestingly, everyone who arrived on the *Lightning* in 1880 reindentured for three or five years as conditions had improved a little by then, and by 1890 all had completed their indenture period. There were no more reports from the Protector of Indians and when the forthcoming visit of Commissioner D.W. Comins to West Indian estates employing indentured Indians was announced for 1891, the St Vincent government advised that it would be unnecessary for no immigrants remained who wished to return to India and no indentured labourers were left.

Post-indenture experience: deculturation and assimilation into the dominant cultural milieu

Cultural and religious practices inherited from India underwent fundamental changes early on in the indenture experience mainly due to the:

- absence of a critical mass of people

- competition among the churches to save the 'heathens'

- estates' attempts to make Indians feel at home in their new environment and to break their ties with their homeland

- absence of special schools for Indian children, who were therefore marginalised in terms of education

Over ninety per cent of the Indians who eventually came to St Vincent were Hindus. By agreement, Indians were allowed to practice their religion, as elsewhere in the West Indies. However, their relatively small number, their dispersion among the estates, and the transient nature of their existence left little scope for their development as a critical demographic mass, and Hinduism could not survive the proselytisation of the Christian churches from the early days of indenture onwards. Infants were baptised in Christian churches and were given Anglo-Saxon names similar to those of the planters, managers and overseers as part of the policy to break their links with India; even young ones who had been born in India were given Anglo-Saxon names. Although they were not forced to change their names, Indians saw it as a way of being accepted in schools and the larger society. Most persons of Indian origin in St Vincent and the Grenadines are now Christians with Anglo-Saxon surnames.

End note

This essay is based on extensive research of documents on Indian indenture in St Vincent, held at The National Archives in London, as well as in the National Archives of St Vincent. In addition, descendants of some who participated in the march of 7 October 1882 recalled stories told to them by their grandparents. Documents consulted at London's National Archive include:

CO 260-CO 384, with particular reference to the Immigration Agents' Reports for the period 1858–90.

Blue Books 1845–90 *(passim).*

In St Vincent the author had access to the Register of Indians held at the time (1994) in a vault at the island's Court House. This document is now housed at the National Archives of St Vincent and the Grenadines.

Further details of the conditions prevailing in St Vincent during the indenture period and prior to the march on Kingstown can be found in:

Arnold Thomas, 'Portuguese and Indian immigration to St. Vincent 1845–1890', *Journal of Caribbean Studies*, 14 (Fall 1999 and Spring 2000): 40–59.

Sita and Jatayu

Lelawattee Manoo-Rahming

It was Jatayu who tried to pursue
Rawan[1] to save Sita, his treasured King's
wife, as she prayed to her Rama to free
her from Rawan's clutch, squeezing tight her spleen.

The Vulture King, Jatayu's time was due.
The demon Rawan's blade had chopped his wings
and, to his friend, Rama granted mukti[2]
as he lay dying in the forest green.

Yet the atman[3] of Jatayu mamoo[4]
calmed the sea, while Sita and her young twins,
in the *Fatel Razack*,[5] crushed and thirsty,
longed for lassi and their royal cuisine.

And wasn't it Jatayu's glance askew
that Sita saw while being weighed from springs
on Nelson Island, then given sari
and a bar of blue soap for her hygiene?

It was Jatayu's steadfastness, like glue,
through the jungles and canefields, and wasp stings,
that feathered Sita as she ate roti
while fighting off brute hands, rough and porcine.

By the light of her bedi,[6] Sita knew
she was tethered strong, even in wind swings,
by Jatayu, anchored in the flame tree,
who shielded her, as if she were still queen.

1   Alternative spellings in diasporic communities for this *Ramayana* character are 'Ravan', 'Ravana' and 'Rawana'.

2   Transcendent state attained as a result of being released from the cycle of rebirth.

3   Soul.

4   Uncle.

5   First ship to bring indentured labourers from India to Trinidad.

6   Hindu earthen altar.

Tales of the Sea[1]

Gaiutra Bahadur

> *and the bones are begging to be let*
> *loose with their drums and handbells,*
> *with their tales of the sea at sunrise.*
> Lauren K. Alleyne, 'Ask No Questions'.

During the week of the Brexit vote, I flew to Thessaloniki from London on the spur of the moment. I was in the United Kingdom on a month-long research trip but had lived there on and off for years, mapping a sea-borne, migrant past in the archives of empire to research my first book. That summer, the summer of 2016, my great-uncle was dying in a hospice in north London. My mood was fragile, and I knew the city far too well. For my sanity, I fled for three days to a little seaside town in Greece, where a friend had been teaching a poetry workshop.

Lauren Alleyne and I had met a few years earlier at a literary festival in Trinidad, and we had become fast friends. Moments after joining her at her hotel outside Thessaloniki, she introduced me to her childhood friend and we three headed straight for the water. We were wading into the Aegean Sea when a group of teenage boys swam over to us. They were friendly, trying out their English, flirting a little perhaps. They told us they were Syrian and had been living in Greece for a few months.

Our own trajectories to that tourist sea, which for some summers had also been a refugee sea, puzzled them. Lauren had grown up in Trinidad but now taught in the American South, in Virginia. Her best friend from high school is also a Trinidadian of African origin but lives and works in Manchester, in the north of England. And I am a Guyanese-American with roots in India, living in New Jersey. Disorienting the boys even further, I offered some broken Arabic remembered from a reporting stint in Iraq.

---

1   This piece is republished with permission from *Griffith Review 59: Commonwealth Now*, January 2018.

The boldest of the boys, the light-eyed one with sandy hair, asked us: 'Are you joined?' It was our turn to be puzzled. Was he asking if we were a couple? Did he want to know how we were connected, across the various geographies and ethnicities we had just claimed? He repeated his question a few more times, with mounting irritation at our failure to comprehend, until finally I said: 'Sure, we're joined. We're friends.'

Ultimately he made us understand that the word he wanted was *enjoying*. The miscommunication nonetheless encouraged some introspection: How were we, actually, joined? And what kind of joining matters? Current events nudged my thoughts in that direction.

As we lay on the beach, our phones alerted us that a majority of Brits had voted to leave the European Union. Only one of us was a British citizen. Yet, we each registered the news as if it were a direct blow. We all were born in former British colonies, and our Facebook feeds buzzed with barbed postcolonial one-liners like: '1947 was the original Brexit!' and 'I wish that Africa had [the] chance to vote remain or Fockoff while the British were pillaging our land.'

Britain, having colonised much of the world, was feeling the chafe of colonisation by Europe. We laughed at the irony because we needed to, because we apprehended the unnerving truth that hostility to immigrants had given Brexit its terrifying charge.

The vote to leave – and the election it foreboded across the Atlantic – revealed a raw, abiding racism under the skin of societies that were supposed to be bending, like the arc of history, towards justice.

Our dismay at Brexit impacted us at an almost cellular level. As immigrants, as people of colour, we felt fear in our very bodies. But there was also something more complicated at work. We also felt a certain sympathy to alliances beyond national borders. Our identities were not as narrow as Guyana or Trinidad, where we were born, or the United States or the United Kingdom, which we had adopted, or even Africa or India, which had given us our skin. Roots – and routes – had mapped us across nation states, both in our own lives and across the generations. Each of our ancestors had been transported to the West Indies in the cargo holds of British ships, across seas not unlike the one we stretched out beside during that girls' trip.

The cosmopolitanism that made us sympathetic to the European Union was born of a traumatic history. We were living in the afterlife of empire. The past wasn't really past. It had left us with an inheritance of harm, but it had also given us an opportunity to belong to something bigger and broader than our immediate origins.

> *Kizi means stay put, but I am yearn: full of drift, of leaving;*
> there is no voyage called return, *I take only the body.*
> Lauren K. Alleyne, 'Ghazal for the Body'.

THERE IS NO voyage called return. My friend borrowed that phrase from the Syrian poet Adonis. And Kizi – the middle name Lauren's mother gave her, trying to lash her to place eighteen years before she left for America – is a character from Alex Haley's *Roots* (Doubleday, 1976), an enslaved woman whose parents were stolen from Africa, who possesses secret knowledge of writing. She uses it to forge a document for her first love to run away. He fails, and the master discovers she can write, leading to the only instance of leaving in her fettered existence, a choiceless one: she is sold off to another plantation, away from her parents, where she is repeatedly raped by her master. Any attempts at love and flight are thwarted. Stay put, she did.

MY GREAT-UNCLE who was dying in London, who did die before the summer was out, believed in Europe. Once an economist for the Commonwealth Secretariat, Uncle Vish was an internationalist. He was a man of the world, but he certainly did not begin that way. He was the son of a rice mill owner who had gone bankrupt, and the grandson of indentured plantation workers. Until he sailed to London, at twenty-one, he had only known an unelectrified coastal stretch of cane and paddy in Guyana's far countryside, on the periphery of the periphery.

Over my many years in and out of London, plunging into archives, I had grown closer to my great-uncle. When I was a child, an ocean away in a working-class American city with a backside view of the Statue of Liberty, he was held up as an icon, a remote symbol of gentility and success. In London, this great-uncle due deference was suddenly talking to me about ideas, as if we were equals, and this endeared him to me. I loved him, also, because I could see my grandmother, his younger sister, in his face. His smile, a kind of sheepish grin, was hers entirely. He would take me to tea, and we would chat about ideas and about his life. His mind ranged over history, politics, international relations. Sometimes, spiritual and philosophical questions preoccupied him. A rational man, suspicious of dogma, he seemed to be trying to work out his own pact with his ancestral Hindu faith.

He would take me to tea at his club along Pall Mall, the spacious avenue hushing everyone and everything with the seriousness of its classical stone facades and the weight of their columns. The Royal Automobile Club was a place where elderly (and overwhelmingly white) gentlemen wearing three-piece suits sat in elegant leather chairs reading *The Times* in the middle of the day. The concierge who took my great-uncle's coat and the waiters who served us salmon sandwiches called him Dr Persaud. He was comfortable in his skin there.

The club was near St James's Square, around the corner from Marlborough House, the old royal residence that serves as headquarters for the Commonwealth Secretariat. It was one of the first places my great-uncle showed me in London. I remember him telling me, at the time, that Prime Minister William Gladstone had often dined there with Queen Victoria. This mattered because the prime minister's father was also the father of indenture. John Gladstone, a sugar planter and parliamentarian, had dreamed up the scheme of transporting indentured Indians to replace emancipated Africans so that his estates in British Guyana wouldn't lose their supply of unfree labour. That my great-uncle, a grandson of 'coolies' ferried across the seas, should put his intellect to work in the house where a Gladstone had done the same was clearly a matter of pride to him.

When the HMS *Hilary* sailed up through the Caribbean Sea and into the Atlantic Ocean in 1954 with my great-uncle Bishnodat Persaud aboard, it was charting a course to the wider world for him. It was freeing him from his provincial origins. At the time, however, that wasn't completely clear to him. At our final RAC Club tea, the October before he died, he confided: 'When I came to London, England was *not* my mother country.' He was a 'country coolie', as the slur went among Guyana's anglicised and overwhelmingly black or Creole urban elite. (Afro-Saxon was the slur in kind.) He lacked capital (social, cultural *and* financial). He had no college degree. Nor was he Christian. London was rough with him during his first years there, the years immediately after the SS *Empire Windrush* landed the first large group of Caribbean immigrants to England. The city was just barely hanging on as an imperial capital when Britain started to see its first significant wave of immigrants from the places it had colonised. They were not just scattered students and seamen but thousands of labourers from the brown and black territories of the Commonwealth, hired to fell forests in Scotland, man factories in Manchester, serve as attendants with the railways in London. Like the rest, Uncle Vish faced discrimination and hardship.

For years, he sold subway tickets on the London Underground. Back home, he had won a copy of *The Collected Works of Shakespeare* for placing first in Junior Cambridge exams, and then he had taught high school, as so many gifted students who lacked the money for higher education overseas did. Everyone believed he had a bright future ahead. They expected him to get a university degree; he would be the first in our family to go to college. But that ambition proved elusive for a long time. Abroad, on that cold distant island, sadness sometimes undid him, and the family had to send his older sister to care for him.

> *... If leaving was your own*
> *doing, if you were captured or borrowed or lost,*
> *if the doors were cast wide or if you pried*
> *them open, if there are doors or doorways –*
> *your name is not a key.*
> Lauren K. Alleyne, 'Eighteen'.

A COMMONWEALTH OPPORTUNITY changed Uncle Vish's fortune. One day, while at a café, he happened to see an ad for a British Council scholarship for students from the territories or former territories of the British empire. The winners were promised not only full tuition and board, but a ticket back to his or her home country. That's how Uncle Vish was able to study economics at Queen's University in Belfast in the late 1950s. The scholarship was a show of soft power, a form of cultural diplomacy after a decade of discontent and dissent from African, Caribbean and South Asian students protesting their treatment in Britain. The hostels for international students were racially segregated and sometimes substandard. Surveillance of student activities intensified over the 1950s, as the British government feared that international student unions and clubs had become hotbeds of anti-colonial activity and communist or even Soviet sympathy.

And indeed London was where the men who would go on to be independence leaders met and mingled as students. Indians met Nigerians met Ghanaians met Jamaicans met Trinidadians, and a decolonisation movement flourished. It was from the capital of empire that the 1948 anti-British uprisings in Accra were plotted, and police searching its architect Kwame Nkrumah's belongings found a membership card for a London branch of the Communist Party. Shridath Ramphal, the Commonwealth secretary-general my great-uncle would serve for two decades, who was born in the same obscure patch of earth as my great-uncle, remembered his own student days in London as a time of churn and cross-pollination (in both ideas and social circles). The movement for federation in the West Indies was born there. As Ramphal recalled in an oral history in 2002, students:

> ceased to be Trinidadians or Jamaicans or Barbadians in London. They were West Indians ... This could never have happened to them in the Caribbean ... They had to be taken out of their island homes, if you like, brought together, to the common realisation of their oneness in the British community – among other things, brought to their common experience of discrimination in the London of those days. They came together in the knowledge that politically, we have to be one in the Caribbean. So Britain was, in fact, the nursery of that whole generation of West Indian politicians who went on to become federal politicians.

Instilling pro-British sentiment in foreign students was a goal from the start, in the 1920s and 1930s, when the students were few, elite and viewed as successor leaders in their home colonies (mimic men, if you will). A thoroughly British education, while lodging with middle-class British families, was supposed to ensure their positive view of British life and inspire collaboration. As the numbers of students skyrocketed, however, their experience of Britain changed. More were coming privately rather than with scholarship support from colonial governments. They didn't always have the resources or the qualifications to adapt. No longer were they seen as temporary guests due British hospitality, but as economic migrants seeking to settle permanently and as rivals for limited places at British universities. During the 1950s, the number of overseas students in Britain multiplied five-fold, and more than two-thirds (about thirty-five thousand) of them were from the self-governing dominions and colonies or former colonies that made up the Commonwealth.

Meanwhile, Britain's influence in the world was on the wane. It was slowly and steadily ceding its empire. And it was beginning to see its future in Europe, in terms of trade. The Commonwealth, sensing its own imminent irrelevance, tried to redefine itself as an international network of educational exchange. It was in that context, beginning in the 1950s, that the British Council offered scholarships to Commonwealth students, to create goodwill toward Britain and counteract any hostile experiences. The Council, the representative of British culture abroad, wasn't officially government but it was paid by government (including the Commonwealth Relations Office) to welcome overseas students and run hostels for them. At the time that Uncle Vish won his scholarship, the British strategy was shifting from funding hostels for foreign students in the UK to promoting the creation of universities in their own colonies and ex-colonies. The explicit expectation was that Commonwealth-funded scholars would go home when they got their degrees. There was, by concerted policy, a voyage called return.

> To go back *is a verb conjugated in dreams,*
> *that dissolves on your tongue when you wake up*
> *Reaching for it. You seek a different debt,*
> *Choose a different peace: your verb,* to forget.
> Lauren K. Alleyne, 'Eighteen'.

IN THE EARLY 1960s, Uncle Vish went home to Guyana with the Trinidadian he met and married in Belfast, and with his older sister – who had only been allowed schooling until the age of eleven in Guyana but had still managed, while anchoring him in London, to earn a sociology degree at an evening polytechnic. He and his sister had perhaps left as 'country coolies' but they had returned as educated elites. They went to work for the government. Guyana was not yet independent, but had limited self-rule under a premier who was the son of plantation workers born in India. That premier was also a Marxist, which led to Anglo-American intervention to undermine him, including CIA-sponsored incitement of tensions between blacks and Indians.

In London, at work on another book as a fellow at the British Library, I wrestled with this material. It added to the weight of my sorrow that summer. At the library, I listened to the late Trevor Carter, an Afro-Trinidadian immigrant to London, describe on tape the political world of guns and guayaberas that he was recruited to in Guyana as a member of the British Communist Party. The Marxist premier's strikingly beautiful Jewish-American wife, meeting Carter at a party in London, had convinced him to go to Guyana to train young cadres in political organising. Her image as 'Mother Courage' had preceded her, and it had been Carter's dream to work full-time for the party in a field where the fight was on. He saw the opportunity as 'very romantic stuff'.

But his years there, 1961–4, were years of scarring interracial violence. Carter described seeing a pregnant young woman lying on the ground outside his rural school with her belly cut open and the baby beside her. She'd been gutted by a cutlass tied around a bamboo spear. He witnessed a bomb explosion at party headquarters in the capital that left a man dead and dismembered. Carter remembered: 'His hands were off, his feet were off.' And the party newspaper he edited turned its printing plant into refugee housing after an ethnically motivated campaign of arson and attacks in an interior mining town displaced its Indian population. 'Man, I saw these people left with nothing, just their clothes, and I saw women who were raped', he recalled. He had gone out to Guyana as an idealist, nurtured in an environment in London where multiple nationalities and races together worked for free, socialist utopias in their home colonies, and the romance he imagined had disintegrated into a nightmare. He left that year.

Uncle Vish, whose time as a junior administrator in the premier's office coincided with Carter's time in Guyana, would not speak to me about what he witnessed. He would only say that 'the troubles', his oblique shorthand for what happened, had left him 'a man without a country.' Had he too taken, like the speaker in Lauren's poem, *only the body* with him back to Guyana? Was his soul stranded somewhere else, transubstantiated, stateless? I imagine that the horror and pettiness of the racial strife he encountered made return impossible. In 1964, he and his wife left Guyana for a university perch in Barbados, where they stayed for a decade until the Commonwealth Secretariat recruited him back to London.

The last time I saw Uncle Vish, I arrived at the hospice just as a Hindu priest who apparently made rounds there was administering last rites. The man touched a drop of holy water to Uncle Vish's lips with a leaf, whispered into his ear, tied a hennaed thread around his wrist and left the room. Uncle Vish, who had not asked for a pundit, fiddled with the red string for an agitated moment. Then, recovering his composure with a chuckle, he made a coolly dismissive comment about Brahmins and their abuses and asked that the thread be removed. His daughter-in-law cut him free from it. Uncle Vish, half a century removed from a rural Hindu past, had no attachments to ritual. He did not believe in caste nor have much use for pundits. One would certainly not be brokering his last voyage.

His generation had experimented with different ways to be joined across race and national origin: through the Commonwealth, the Communist Party, the anti-colonial struggle, the non-aligned movement, even the chimera of a federated West Indies. They had bequeathed to us models that were political or economic in nature. But a common history of colonisation by the British, as well as shared resistance to that colonisation, has not ended misapprehension and tension between blacks and Indians in both Guyana and Trinidad.

> *Tonight you are full of small rivers:*
> *Your eyes salty runoff, the rust-bright*
> *Trickle staining your thigh, the unnameable*
> *Undammed flooding in your chest*
> *You are drowning in all of them. Sweet girl,*
>
> ...
>
> *Some rivers are wider than any courage.*
> *I give you nothing as you sink, alone*
> *Under those waters. This is how I am born.*
>
> *Under those waters you labour to birth me.*
> Lauren K. Alleyne, 'Eighteen'.

FOR LAUREN AND I, the ways we are joined are feats against the geopolitical. Ours is a league of letters, without member states, defying mapping. Our bonds are aesthetic – and aquatic. We both draw from a fluid imaginary based in bodies of water, in death and birth on water.

Rivers run through Lauren's first volume of poetry, *Difficult Fruit* (Peepal Tree Press, 2014). Her epigraph, from Lucille Clifton's 'Female', prepares the reader: 'There is an amazon in us.' But is that supposed to reassure or terrify us? Allusions to seas, oceans and rivers inundate Lauren's verses. That's not particularly surprising;

she did call a Caribbean island home until moving to the US at the age of eighteen. What's striking is the warring way that she invokes water. In 'Eighteen', a poem about rape, the sweet girl is drowning but she gives birth – to the speaker, it would seem. *Under those waters you labour to birth me.* Are the speaker and the sweet girl she addresses one: a divided self simultaneously destroyed and created in one moment, by one act of violence?

Her poem summons for me a Middle Passage mythological site: Drexciya, the fantasy land dreamed up by an eponymous 1990s African-American techno duo as a setting for their songs. As they imagined it, this underwater world arose from acts of violence recuperated: enslaved pregnant women thrown overboard by slave traders gave birth to a race of aquatic humanoids, adapted to submarine existence in the Atlantic terrain where slave ships crossed. Human drowning during human trafficking provides the backdrop for a creation story that the musicians elaborate on across their oeuvre.

Slave traders threw pregnant women, among other captives, overboard to claim insurance money for the loss of their lives. Indenture was a successor form of trafficking, transporting half a million Indians to the Caribbean to replace freed slaves on plantations from 1838 to 1917. Like slave voyages, indenture voyages provided a stage for high mortality, sexual assault and suicide. But pregnant indentured women were not thrown overboard; unlike slave traders, their traffickers were apparently paid enough per head to land each alive.

Pregnant 'coolie' women did, however, occasionally *jump* overboard. During one archival dive, I netted the story of Ramratia, who disappeared on a voyage to British Guiana in 1894 while four months pregnant. As her ship was towed downriver in Calcutta, the surgeon aboard reported that Ramratia had complained of a pain in her belly. She was afraid of miscarrying. A few days later, she was nowhere to be found aboard *The Avoca* and was presumed to have jumped overboard. While crossing the *kala pani* (Hindi for the dark waters between India and the New World), she apparently felt a foreboding in her womb and exercised what choice she could to abort all – the voyage, the pregnancy, the seas of uncertainty ahead. As she sank, alone, to what might she have given birth? Where might speculative fancy lead us? Are there parallel Drexciyas to invent from the drownings of these other expecting mothers?

The Guyanese-Canadian poet Arnold Itwaru saw 'Shiva's unending dance' at work during the crossings. And indeed Shiva, the Hindu god who destroys in order to create, who dances in a ring of flames to maintain the universe's ceaseless cycle of creation and destruction, did not forget the cargo holds confining the indentured. Surgeons aboard the ships prepared balance sheets of births and deaths, tallying the human gain and loss on each voyage. My own great-grandmother was pregnant when she sailed to Guiana in 1903, as were eleven per cent of the women on her ship. My grandfather was born, legs first, on the Atlantic, a debut said to have endowed him with a healer's magic. On indenture voyages, birth and death were not just physically constant. They were metaphysically large.

In the tales the indentured told, they spoke of crossing seven seas, seven shades of water, shades of darkness and light, light that died and darkness that was born, darkness somehow extinguished and light rekindled. They mythologised the point where the Indian Ocean collided with the Atlantic Ocean as the *pagal samundar*, or the mad seas, investing it with almost supernatural meaning. Entering it, somewhere around the Cape in southern Africa, is a pivotal plot point in the creation story of my people.

This is how I have retold the tale: *The captain's wheel became Shiva's fiery circle, turning and turning in its cosmic spiral. And in the gyrating of the gales, and the churning of the waves, as one steered and the other danced, we became new.*

Uprooted, most had to recreate family during passages from India that significantly obliterated Hindu/Muslim as well as caste barriers. People who had left behind uncles, sisters, husbands and mothers substituted their fellow travellers for kin. For the indentured, return was a promise made in writing, part of their contract; but only a quarter ever journeyed back to India. Many who did found themselves rejected by their families and neighbors in their native villages. They had lost the moorings of caste. By Hindu orthodoxy, the very act of crossing the seas had turned them into polluted and polluting beings. Countless numbers languished in riverside slums in Calcutta while clamouring for boats to take them away from India yet again. For the overwhelming majority of 'coolies', there would be no return.

In our beginning, there was a boat. Having emerged from its belly, as survivors, indentured Indians could no longer be who they had been.

Like the slaves before them, they were an entirely new people, forged by suffering, created through destruction.

Those who made the three-month crossing together in the bellies of boats called each other *jahaji bhai*, which in Hindi means 'boat brother', or *jahaji behen*, which means 'boat sister'. Half a century after my great-grandmother gave birth on *The Clyde*, she still held court in her yard, smoking a tobacco pipe and gossiping with women who had travelled on that same ship with her. For decades, her jahaji behen would come from many miles away to visit her in her village in Guiana, and she returned the kindness.

The Middle Passage created new kinship ties for the enslaved, as well. Scholars of eighteenth-century Atlantic slavery have written about the bond that developed between slaves who braved the crossings on the same ship, a bond equal to blood ties because in many cases it had to replace blood ties. This, after all, was a group of people who had been wrenched from their families and their clans. 'Shipmate' became its own kinship category once slaves were in their new worlds, and it survived from one generation to the next. In Haiti, the word used for someone who crossed on the same ship was *batiment*; in Trinidad, it was *malongue*. And in Surinam, it was *mati*. In the case of both the indentured and the enslaved, there was a particular intimate word to call out someone who had made the journey on the same ship with you.

It's possible to make the concepts of ship sister and shipmate more symbolic and malleable, so that every descendant of indenture is a jahaji and every descendant of slavery a shipmate. An even more radical step in redefinition might also be taken. The courageous and the imaginative have ventured it – for one, the Trinidadian calypsonian Brother Marvin, who identifies as black but has Indian ancestors. In his 1990s hit 'Jahaji Bhai', he sang of his *bahut aja*, his great-grandfather, who had come from Calcutta to plant sugar-cane and thereby had made Indo-Caribbeans the calypsonian's jahaji bhai. Brother Marvin reimagined a brotherhood of the boat that would ally Indian and African as kin, forged by parallel historical traumas. And just so, I could have told the Syrian boy in the Aegean that waterborne pasts still sending out ripples, giving us our figurative language, connect me to Lauren and Lauren to me. We *are* joined. We are ship sisters in our creative vocabularies.

> *Four naked women stand waist-deep*
> *in the Aegean, laughter unchained*
> *from their throats. They consecrate the sea.*
> Lauren K. Alleyne, '10 Most Sacred Spots on Earth'.

ON 23 DECEMBER 2015, a wooden boat capsized in the Aegean Sea on its way to Greece. The Turkish coastguard rescued twenty-one people but twenty others died, including a pregnant woman. News agencies never reported her name, let alone who she was. Her story drowned with her. In the past three years, more than a million refugees, most fleeing shattering conflict in Syria, have taken her particular route to freedom: the fragile hour's crossing from the Turkish coast of the Aegean to various Greek islands and Europe beyond. More than eleven hundred of them have died in the attempt; this woman was but one anonymous casualty. And she was far from the only woman with child among the displaced millions made into scapegoats by nativist politicians across Europe, breeding Brexit and other backlashes. One in ten refugees is pregnant. Many give birth and within a day march onward. Human smugglers reportedly have made it a tactic to throw pregnant women and children overboard when merchant ships approach, gambling on a humanitarian intervention. How many sink, unrescued? And what can possibly be born from their unmemorialised ends under those waters? Are there any alternative worlds, any creation myths, imaginable from their nameless deaths?

The summer I visited Greece, fifty thousand refugees were living there, mainly in four camps. The light-eyed boy with the sandy hair and the provocative question might have been one of them. He and his mates, satisfied that we were enjoying ourselves, swam off on their own that day. We were left wading and wondering about the encounters the seas enable, in their haunted ebb.

Pot-bellied Sardar

David Dabydeen

(for Maria del Pilar Kaladeen and Tina K. Ramnarine)

The ship had live duckling, hen and fowlcock
But the salt mutton spoil with worm and rat.
Peas stay good though and rain top up the vat.
They feed me full-full and I never thirst.
As Chief, and charged with duty, *my* plate first.
By the time we reach Berbice[1] homestretch
I feast so much my belly close to burst.
Brimful, then more, a lesser man would retch.

Swallow the food, the dhall and rice a slurry!
Hold up your finger to the sun and lick
The last dribble or flake of fish curry
To show jahiji bhai[2] who is boss man,
Not white Captain, white crew, but Sadiq Khan!
As proof I put on this much extra fat,
All day slacken and rebind dhōti,
Loose it, make it fit, knot this way and that,
So all-body see I is Nawab Roti,
I is Goat-stew Babu and Ghee Malik :
True-true, plenty I eat to the point of sick...
Is so with Leaders, gravy always thick.

1   Region in Guyana.
2   The concepts of Jahaji Bhai and Jahaji Bahen meaning 'ship brother/sister' refer to
    the bonds forged by people who made friendships on the boat journey, said to be
    so strong that your jahaji bhai's children were like cousins to your own children,
    so descendants would frown on intermarriage.

SCHOOL OF ADVANCED STUDY | **UNIVERSITY OF LONDON**

The School of Advanced Study unites nine institutes at the University of London to form the UK's national centre for the pursuit, support and promotion of research in the humanities.

The institutes of the School publish a wide range of titles across different disciplines, including:

In Protest: 150 Poems for Human Rights
edited by Helle Abelvik-Lawson, Anthony Hett and Laila Sumpton
2013 ● 978-0-9575210-3-2 ● £15.00
In Protest: 150 Poems for Human Rights is an anthology of new poetry exploring human rights and social justice themes. This collection, a collaboration between the Human Rights Consortium at the School of Advanced Study, University of London, and the Keats House Poets, brings together writing that is often very moving, frequently touching, and occasionally humorous. The 150 poems included here come from over 16 countries, and provide a rare insight into experiences of oppression, discrimination, and dispossession – and yet they also offer strong messages of hope and solidarity. This anthology brings you contemporary works that are truly outstanding for both their human rights and poetic content.

Envisioning Global LGBT Human Rights: (Neo)colonialism, Neoliberalism, Resistance and Hope
edited by Nancy Nicol, Adrian Jjuuko, Richard Lusimbo, Nick Mulé, Susan Ursel, Amar Wahab and Phyllis Waugh
forthcoming 2018 ● 978-0-9931102-3-8 ● £25.00
Envisioning Global LGBT Human Rights: (Neo)colonialism, Neoliberalism, Resistance and Hope is an outcome of a five-year international collaboration among partners that share a common legacy of British colonial laws that criminalise same-sex intimacy and gender identity/expression. The project sought to facilitate learning from each other and to create outcomes that would advance knowledge and social justice. The project was unique, combining research and writing with participatory documentary video film-making. This visionary politics infuses the pages of the anthology.

To order or to see the full range of titles published by the institutes of the School, please visit www.sas.ac.uk/publications/.

Lightning Source UK Ltd.
Milton Keynes UK
UKHW010058151218
334029UK00006B/372/P